NO JERKS
ON THE JOB

ANSHI,

DON'T TAKE NO GUFF!

NO JERKS ON THE JOB

Take Back Control of Your Workplace

Ron Newton

BROWN BOOKS
PUBLISHING GROUP

No Jerks on the Job
Take Back Control of Your Workplace

Brown Books Publishing Group
16250 Knoll Trail Drive, Suite 205
Dallas, Texas 75248
www.BrownBooks.com
(972) 381-0009
A New Era in Publishing®

ISBN 978-1-61254-899-9
Library of Congress Control Number 2016930877

Printed in the United States
10 9 8 7 6 5 4 3 2 1

For more information or to contact the author, please go to
www.NoJerksOnTheJob.com.

To my wife, Melanie, the love of my life.

Contents

Introduction

Is American business in trouble today because of "people problems" caused by jerks on the job? You know it is if you have turned on the news and heard about another major company going belly-up, another executive being investigated for corruption, another report showing workplace infighting, employee disloyalty, and ethical violations at all levels. And just as likely—or so I'm willing to bet—you know about the "jerks on the job" problem because you are facing it in your own workplace.

Perhaps you've seen a manager in your company quit in disgust at the shenanigans of his employees, leaving the company with a hefty price tag for replacing him. Or maybe productivity in your business has taken a dive because so many leaders and other workers are refusing to pull their own weight. Then again, you may have serious concerns about the cutting of ethical corners and the potential for criminal offenses being committed in your workplace. In our twenty-first-century business world, such problems are common in companies large and small, blue collar and white.

These problems worry you, threaten your company's viability, and spoil the pleasure you take in your work. Yet you may not know where to turn for help. You may not even be able to define what has hit you. All you know is that you are frustrated. Your workplace is hurting because of toxic employees who don't seem to know what it means to be responsible adults, and you want to know what to do about it.

I'm more than willing to help with that. As president of the independent consulting agency PEAK Training Solutions, I have helped leaders in businesses all across the land solve problems caused by jerks on the job. I am eager to share these proven answers with you in *No Jerks on the Job* so that, whether you are an executive, a manager, or a regular employee, you can start to turn things around.

I got these answers years ago from a surprising place—the wilderness trail where I spent countless days with teenage offenders who had been ordered by the court system to attend the camp program I was then running.

Brats Grown Up

Who would have thought that solutions to today's business crisis of personal immaturity would come from juvenile delinquents? Certainly not me, at least not before 1992. It was then that businesspeople began to approach me, asking if what I had learned about helping troubled kids could be applied to their dysfunctional employees. The difference was, they weren't talking about an isolated individual or two; they were describing a large part of their labor force. As you will discover in these pages, the problem is now even worse.

I have a special name for today's jerks on the job. I call them "adult brats" because they're just like the troubled youths I worked with years ago. In fact, they *are* such juvenile delinquents, now grown up (at least chronologically) and making trouble in workplaces all across the country.

Today, I still derive a slightly perverse pleasure when I stand before corporate or industry groups and tell them that troubled kids taught me the solution to their employees' behavioral problems. At first, the reaction of people in the audience is to laugh nervously while glancing sideways at someone else. Then, as if choreographed, heads begin to nod in agreement—a recognition that today's business problems stem more from character issues than from poor policies or procedures. It seems as if everybody knows an adult brat.

I never intended for my success in helping troubled kids to translate into strategies to save businesses inundated with "people problems," but because it did, I'm delighted to share those tactics with you. Let me say that it's not as if I possessed a magic cure in working with youths or was perfect in my own behavior back then; I made plenty of mistakes. Still, I persevered in my work for twenty years, helping more than twelve hundred troubled teens and preadolescents in what was one of the nation's first full-time wilderness therapy camp programs. That was the foundation of the success I've helped to instigate in business after business.

As you progress through this book, you will realize that I'm taking you on a wilderness journey similar to the ones I led years ago. Using this ongoing metaphor is the best way for me to describe the core principles that will counter the influence of those troubled employees who seek to destroy your work environment and business effectiveness. I hope you will also find that it makes for an entertaining format, resulting in a business book with a unique flavor.

In telling stories from the wilderness camp, I have protected the privacy of the youths, as well as of my wilderness staff and other adult trip participants, by altering their names. Similarly, I've used pseudonyms for the names of both companies and employees in several instances where I tell stories from the business world. But trust me in this: it's all real. Just as real as the problems you are dealing with in your company.

What To Look For

If you are undecided about the extent of the harm done to business by the increasing number of jerks on the job—or adult brats—in the workplace, Part 1 of this book should convince you that it's done a great deal of harm indeed. You'll also find out how we as Americans got our business sector into the spot where it is today.

In Part 2, you'll find answers for the problems adult brats are causing in American business. I'll take you past the "make nice" offered by so many of today's employee counselors and down the difficult trail to solutions that work permanently.

My friend, the jerks don't have to win. You can take back your workplace, and your victory begins now.

PART ONE

The Problem

---

*Liars, Thieves, and the
Just Plain Rotten*

Chapter One

Help! I'm Surrounded by Jerks!

The ringing of the telephone disrupted the peace of my Colorado camp office one day in 1992. For several years, the office had been my headquarters as I organized and led wilderness trips to rehabilitate delinquent youth. Looking out my window at the beautiful Sangre de Cristo mountain range as I reached for the phone that day, I was totally unprepared for the direction the call would take—and the new direction it would give to my life.

"Are you the camp program that helps troubled kids?" asked the voice on the other end of the line.

"Yes," I replied.

"Good. I have some for you—they're my employees."

My caller identified himself as Art Rollins, the general manager of a trucking company. Art proceeded to tell me that his drivers were acting irresponsibly, dragging morale down to a level that affected safety performance and caused high rates of personnel turnover. Nothing he had tried seemed to stop their dangerous, immature behavior. He needed help, and he needed it soon, before one of his truckers precipitated more than a crisis of immaturity.

I had heard the same type of complaint and plea for help hundreds of times before—from parents and authorities talking about delinquent youngsters. It was uncanny how much Art's employees sounded like the kids who participated in my camp program. But, until I heard Art's plea for help, it had never dawned on me that corporate America needed what I was doing to help troubled youth.

My curiosity was piqued. Was Art's business really filled with troubled adolescents in adult bodies? And if so, was his company a rare case, or were there many other businesses in the same situation all across the land? There was only one way to find out, and so I answered yes to Art's plea.

EYE-OPENER

One of Art's first assignments for me was to interview a driver involved in a truck accident. Art suspected the driver was being less than truthful in his account of the incident. Art wanted to know, "Is my guy lying?" Beneath this blunt request, there was a deeper, unspoken appeal—a colossal question similar to one that parents of troubled youth often asked me: "How do I get him to stop?" Except in Art's case, it was, *How do I get a bunch of them to stop?*

The trucking company's dispatch room reeked of ego as I listened to the trucker trying to convince me that he was telling the truth about the accident. To Art, the young driver represented his worst nightmare: the combination of developed job talent and undeveloped personal maturity. Art knew his company's profits depended on the former but were endangered by the latter.

As the trucker nervously chattered away, I looked out the window. There sat a crumpled semitrailer, a piece of equipment he had been pulling northbound on a narrow two-lane road until a southbound truck of similar size sideswiped him—or so he claimed. It sounded plausible to me. Then again, the trucker could have claimed that Santa's sleigh hit him and I wouldn't have known the difference. Until that time, I had never been in a commercial trucking dispatch room, and I knew little about trucking rules of the road.

Given my ignorance, I kept reminding myself why I was there in the first place: to find the truth. Art felt his employees were beginning to act less like responsible adults and more like untrustworthy juvenile delinquents, and I knew all about troubled youth. Exposing their deceptive nature was my expertise; restoring them to responsible behavior was my calling.

True to Art's suspicion, the more the trucker talked, the more he sounded like a wildly deceptive teenager in my wilderness program for troubled kids. "My job is the toughest on the planet; it takes a lot of skill, plus knowing how a narrow road affects the handling of a big rig like mine," he said. "Why, airline pilots have it easier than me. I can land a Boeing 747, but a 747 pilot can't drive my rig and do my job. Let one of them try to squeeze my big rig into the tiny spaces they give me. I'll take a runway any day."

A man who said this would lie about anything.

Adult Brats

If the trucker's behavior were an isolated case, it could be dismissed as a bad hire. But I find that many managers across industry boundaries agree with Art. The emotional maturity and moral veracity of today's workforce—employee honesty, loyalty, compassion, teamwork, patience—have declined steadily, exposing the workplace to aberrant employee behaviors that derive from a substantial erosion of personal values. In turn, this lack of personal values is reflected in a growing number of soulless businesspeople and business practices, annually costing businesses billions of dollars in revenue. Some of this loss is publicly evident and counted; but much of it, like the effects of Art Rollins's dishonest truck driver, exists in the uncounted squalor of jerks on the job who behave as if there are no rules in life.

My term for workers who exhibit the character of delinquent adolescents is *adult brats*. Jerks on the job are adult brats. By creating this name, I am saying in effect that it is okay, in fact crucial, to identify and talk about these workers. If we do not, then we choose to naively ignore the foremost management crisis facing American business today: the harmful influence of an increasing number of emotionally adolescent, irresponsible adults in the workplace.

Like the kids who attended my camps, adult brats act irresponsibly. They have difficulty seeing beyond their noses. Though they may be far into adulthood chronologically, adult brats live in an emotional state of prolonged adolescence; and as adults, they attempt to get away with behavior that a teenager might think is justified. The problem is, teenagers are thinking impaired.

Bernard Madoff of Bernard L. Madoff Investment Securities LLC, Lois Lerner of the Internal Revenue Service, Franklin Raines of Fannie Mae, Angelo R. Mozilo of Countrywide Corporation, Henry T. Nicholas III of Broadcom Corporation, Jeffrey Skilling of Enron, and many other business leaders who have been dragged before the courts of law or of public opinion were adult brats.

So were many of the truckers in Art Rollins's company, as I found out during my consulting time with them.

As are, probably, some of the people you know. In fact, I'll bet you understand just what I mean when I refer to adult brats. Or do you?

A Deep, Dark Problem

Art thought he understood adult brats, but like many business professionals, he saw only the surface behaviors that cost his company money. Like a parent overwhelmed by the moment-to-moment struggle to cope with a disobedient child, he didn't have the emotional energy to look for deeper issues. He suspected there was more to it—root causes and such—but he couldn't see them. You can't take action on what you can't see or define.

Anyone with discerning eyes can detect the growing divide between responsible workers and irresponsible workers in today's business world. But the adult brat problem runs deeper and darker than responsible versus irresponsible, good work ethic versus bad, or any single measure you can use to judge personal maturity and sound values. The problem extends to the root cause of the divide, begging us to examine the sociological forces that produce adult brats and to determine what, if anything, we can do to stop these behavioral patterns. This is not an easy task and there are no quippy answers. I won't give you any facile promises; it's not in my nature. I didn't take delinquents on the camp trail to hold hands and sing "Kum Ba Yah," and Art's employees never mistook me for a touchy-feely counselor.

American business is in crisis because our society is at its deepest dividing point. Now more than ever before, people entering the workforce have a clear-cut moral choice in their career path: join the ranks of the troubled youth in adult bodies or follow the lead of mature adults. The crisis confronting American business has come about because today more new workers are inclined to do the former rather than the latter. We'll talk more about this later.

You may think that I sound jaded, a bit like my father's generation—the "greatest generation." By saving the free world and building the United States into the greatest socioeconomic force in world history, his generation thought they had invented the rule book—black-and-white rules, no gray—that governs all behavior. (I still bear the stab marks from my dad's fork, a teaching tool he used to "encourage" me to get my elbows off the dining table.) Sadly, like many of his generation, he died a pessimist, thinking that successive generations were causing the world to go to hell in a handbasket.

That's not me, and I hope it's not you. I remain an optimist, with the same vision of hope that propelled me to invest my early life in a wilderness camp program that helped more than a thousand change-resistant troubled youth.

But I'm also a realist, and the demonstrative language I use in our conversation portrays nothing less than the real choices about conduct in the workplace that every employee must face. Your choices are to be an adult brat, fight the adult brat, or ignore the adult brat at your own risk and that of your company. Art Rollins chose to fight with me at his side, and two years later, when the battle was over, he had saved his small company more than $250,000 in personnel turnover and safety-related costs. He could also sleep soundly at night, knowing the dependable character of his employees.

The choice for people entering a new work environment is illustrated in the case of Billy Taylor, a new employee. I visited him at his workplace, a communications equipment service center with low morale and a high personnel turnover rate.

BILLY

Billy was a twenty-one-year-old lab technician with some college credits. He was well spoken and, by all reports, a good worker who would soon be on the rise. I first met Billy three months after he had started his job, and I was anxious to ask him about his reaction to his coworkers. But I never had the opportunity. Why? Because I was constantly distracted by Billy's overbearing, braggart supervisor—Jake Nyland, an attention-grabbing human vacuum cleaner.

The man was omnipresent. Every time I turned around during my three-day visit to Billy's workplace, Jake was there to tell me something about himself. The more he revealed, the more I mentally checked my list of past wilderness trip participants. Hadn't I seen Jake before? The garble of ego-driven claims and half-truths that poured from his mouth made me think so.

Jake's list of self-proclaimed feats was seemingly endless:

- Hard worker. Longest serving worker. Best worker in the company.
- Good cook. Gourmet cook. Turned down offers to be a chef because he likes his current job.
- Landowner. Ranch owner. Charitably gave ranch to elderly parents because he works so many hours on his job that he can't care for the ranch.
- Dedicated worker. Won't tolerate a lack of dedication in any other worker. Divorced wife because she couldn't understand his dedication to his job.

On and on Jake went as he made it clear that he would let nothing stand in the way of his doing his job as he saw fit.

During the last day of my visit, I finally grabbed some one-on-one time with Billy in the company's break room. My conversation with the quiet, polite young man confirmed everything I had been told about him. He was a keeper, the kind of employee you want to develop into a future leader. Then his supervisor walked into the room, and the vacuum cleaner turned himself on again.

Brag after brag proceeded from Jake's mouth, but this time he used Billy as his foil. "I've tried to teach this guy a thing or two," he said as he pointed to Billy, "but he won't listen. I guess he's going to have to learn the hard way."

More jabs at Billy followed, but Billy remained quiet, lowering his head while shaking it slowly. To me, it looked as if he was about to explode. Or vomit. Instead, though, he looked my way from his bowed position, pointed to his boss, and asked me a simple question. "Am I going to turn out to be like him?"

What a profound question! This young man discerned that his supervisor represented something deeply wrong in the workplace, something that could drastically affect him as he traveled his career path. By turning to me, Billy, like Art Rollins, was asking for insight into what he should do when caught in a workplace with adolescent-like employees such as Jake, a worker of questionable character.

A Question Of Character

More than three decades ago, a close friend introduced me to an old adage: "The measure of a man's character is what it takes to stop him." Because I share the same personal values as my friend, the obvious question never occurred to me: "Stop him from doing what?" I assumed the answer was to stop him from stepping into bad character, defined as behavior outside the bounds allowed by our personal values.

The meaning of the old adage isn't as obvious now; its frame of reference has become oblique. Personal value systems have never been more diverse, leading to a moral relativism that makes it nearly impossible for business to establish an acceptable measure of employee character. One person's moral giant at work can be another's immoral dwarf, but you can't say much about it, even if you suspect the dwarf of corporate cannibalism.

Given the climate of moral relativity, I could have returned Billy's question ("Am I going to turn out to be like him?") with some politically correct therapeutic gobbledygook designed to surface his feelings about Jake. I could have asked Billy why he didn't like Jake's personal value system. Or I could have told him why he was wrong to so quickly eliminate Jake as a potential role model.

Similarly, when Art Rollins called, I could have dismissed his concern and told him to take it easy on the young driver whose character was in development. "It's just a phase of life that every young man passes through," I might have said. "Besides, many men his age have trouble with total honesty. Who are you to say such struggle is bad?"

But those weren't the answers Billy and Art wanted from me. They wanted me to define what the measure of an employee's behavior should be (just as I defined the measure of acceptable behavior for troubled kids on my wilderness trips) and then somehow make the employee live up to it. They wanted me to redefine acceptable character because the adult brats in their workplace had rewritten whatever description once existed. That's what adult brats do—they exploit weak systems of behavioral control to redefine acceptable character at their own comfort level. This runs contrary to the very meaning of character.

Plutarch said, "Character is simply long habit continued." He wasn't far off. The definition of our word *character* comes from a Latin root word with virtually the same spelling. It means "an instrument for branding." The Latin term in turn derives from the Greek word *kharakter*, meaning "engraved mark," or brand.[1]

Don't get lost in the language; look where it points. Character implies the manufacture of the same image or product time and time again, the consistency of marking or branding that guarantees the product is genuine and acceptable. In today's business vernacular, the concept is called *quality assurance*.

Having good character means you haven't changed from the measure (quality) of good character that came before you. And the measure that came before that. And before that. With good character, deviance is not allowed.

Adult brats love debilitating deviance. They are exactly like the troubled kids I worked with for twenty years. As those kids showed me, the only way to solve adult brat problems faced by responsible employees like Billy and Art is to help them do the tough things necessary to build personal character in problem employees. I've had plenty of practice helping businesses stop the adult brat-led deviance that destroys the essence of good corporate conduct.

Call me a "bratbuster" if you like, not that I've always been of impeccable character myself. I readily confess that I learned much about my own personal foibles in the process of helping troubled kids. But remember who is really talking to you in this book. It's the thousand troubled kids who taught me all you need to know about character. I'll share those lessons—solutions—with you later in this book.

Hitting The Trail

Before heading out on our journey to discover the solutions to the most compelling crisis in the American workplace, I need to ask you a few questions. They are the same questions I asked many troubled kids who sat in my office, feeling helpless to fight the personal character demons that hounded them. Only, you need to frame them in reference to your willingness to stop the insanity of adult brat behavior that may stalk you in your workplace.

First, do you really want to go on this trip with me? Really?

Second, do you want to battle the heat, cold, sweat, rain, hail, snow, swollen streams, poorly prepared food rations, heavy loads, oxygen deprivation, sore muscles, aggravating campmates, and demanding counselors so that you can learn the life-changing solutions for the personal problems that threaten your success in life?

Be forewarned. The journey we take together in this book, like the wilderness trips I conducted, is not easy. Before the solutions are examined, the ugly story of the way in which many of today's workers became more of a liability than an asset must be told. As a professor of mine, Howard Hendricks, used to state, "There is no implementation without, first, evaluation." Evaluating ourselves and our companies, like checking my middle-age weight at the doctor's office, can be painful and embarrassing.

If you're like Billy and Art and are open to seeking the answers to some hard-hitting questions, then put on your backpack filled with employee problems, relationship issues, ethical shortcomings, and any other labor issues that hinder your work process. Follow me down the trail to solutions. Just remember, whatever insights I give you in this book, I first learned from troubled kids. Got any in your workplace?

Chapter Two

Selling Us Out

Did you decide to hike down the trail with me? Good. I'm going to take it as a given that you are not an adult brat and that you want your business to avoid suffering the poisonous effects brought on by jerks on the job. You may be a CEO, a middle manager, or an entry-level employee; you may belong to a mammoth corporation or you may be working in a mom-and-pop shop; you may have been part of the workforce for a long time; or you may be new to the business world. Regardless, you have something in common with me and with many others in the American workforce: you have been personally touched in some way by the growing presence of adult brats in the workplace.

In recent years, these problems have gotten far worse. Our technology has improved, our information sources have expanded, and our reach has gone global; but the most essential element for business success—the human being on the job—has been causing more difficulties than ever before.

People tend to think about these problems in terms of individuals and their individual behaviors. Thus companies typically conduct investigations on a case-by-case basis, such as Art Rollins initially asked me to do. Though it's easier to identify the isolated behavior of jerks on the job, the cumulative effect of several of them working together in any business operation cannot be overstated. Not every business has felt the acute effects of this crisis yet. (SPM Communications, a public relations firm in the Dallas area, openly advertises a "jerk-free environment" hiring policy.)[1] But this crisis is already consuming other companies.

Graywater Marine, Inc., a now-defunct inland marine company, could have been a poster child for immature and unethical employees, with the motto "All jerks welcome." Because I learned firsthand about the flawed human core that contributed to its demise, I am using its story to show how severe the cumulative effect of adult brats can become.

FRANK AND JERRY

On an evening in November 1994, along a notorious stretch of Louisiana waterway called the Forked Island wiggles, two Graywater Marine vessel officers piloting the towboat MV (motor vessel) *Fortune* demonstrated just how quickly the lack of character can lead to a surrender of the business soul.

The officers—Frank Goodwin and Jerry Broussard—were both highly experienced. The MV *Fortune* was a towboat (mistakenly called tugboat)—a flat-bottomed motor vessel that pushes barges. Goodwin and Broussard belonged to a particularly proud fraternity of towboaters: those who ply their trade primarily along the nerve-racking narrow canal known as the Gulf Intracoastal Waterway.

Compounding the difficulty of the towboaters' job are places along the canal called *wiggles*, where the canal meanders in agonizingly tight turns, creating blind spots and a hazardous turning radius. As Jerry Broussard told me, a wiggle tests more than a towboater's navigational skill; it demands every ounce of his emotional and physical fiber.

As you might expect, wiggles are unsafe places where numerous groundings and collisions occur. Indeed, no towboater realistically expects to complete a career of navigating the wiggles without a scrape, grounding, or collision on his record. Not surprisingly, then, it was in the Forked Island wiggles near Kaplan, Louisiana, that Frank Goodwin grounded the lead barge of his gasoline-filled towing unit in November 1994. What happened next, though, was unforgivable. Neither Frank nor Jerry reported the grounding, as required by law. Instead, they freed the barge from its unwanted mooring, discovered that no gasoline had spilled from the grounded barge, and continued down the canal as if nothing had happened. Human error compounded human error.

RECIPE FOR DISASTER

It's not as if Graywater Marine didn't know that it had a potential crisis of dysfunctional employee behavior on its hands. Earlier in 1994, the general manager of Graywater Marine asked me to ride his company's vessels and develop a personality profile for each vessel officer. The primary goal of the profile was to assist each officer in understanding his behavioral strengths and weaknesses, particularly in areas that affected his ability to develop safety teamwork aboard the vessel. The personality data I collected also was used to develop a baseline portrait of the behavioral culture of Graywater Marine's entire organization, operational shore staff included.

Each officer's profile contained specific recommendations to Graywater for the personal and professional development of the officer. This is what I told them about Frank and Jerry:

FRANK: "Frank is a reluctant leader and is basically a conflict avoider. This means he has a tendency to lead only when he has to. He tends to lead in reacting to a crisis or conflict rather than anticipating it and addressing it through proactive leadership. . . . He has asked for leadership training."

JERRY: "Jerry's weaknesses are related to his reluctance to be assertive with his leadership capabilities, or to actually employ his communication skills. These are due to his overly submissive nature."

Both men were reluctant leaders, not suited for command. Together, they constituted a recipe for disaster that was enabled by operational managers who ignored the reports I submitted. One reason for their ignorance is that the operational managers were the product of value-challenged ownership and senior leadership. More about that in a moment.

Given what I had learned about these two vessel officers in my profiling, their reaction to the barge's grounding was predictable. Frank, the "conflict avoider" first captain, suggested to his "overly submissive" second captain, Jerry, that they violate the law to avoid a run-in with their shore-based supervisor. To Jerry, Frank's plan sounded acceptable, and so they did not communicate an incident report.

What is amazing is that these two veteran vessel officers, like misbehaving schoolkids who weren't caught in the act, thought they could get away with their misbehavior. More amazing is their perception of Graywater's management. Did the men think the company leadership was weak and ineffectual and therefore easy to fool? Or that it would approve of their aberrant behavior with a wink? You can imagine them thinking, *They'll never find out. They'll believe anything we say. We can get away with it.*

They didn't get away with it. Less than seventy-two hours after passing Forked Island, one of the deck crew noticed a trickle of gasoline rising to the water's surface from beneath the lead barge. The trickle was not enough to cause a sheen on the river's surface but was enough to cause concern. Within a few miles, the trickle had grown into a leak too obvious to ignore. From the leak came a pour; from the pour came more than the conflict that Frank and Jerry had initially sought to avoid.

Both men were well intentioned and seemingly dedicated to the job, but prone to make poor, unethical judgments because of a fundamental lack of personal character. In their desire to escape responsibility, they wishfully overlooked the high probability that the grounding had created a below-surface crack in the barge. In fact, that is exactly what had happened. The crack had been filled by hard clay as the barge made contact with the canal bottom, preventing gasoline from leaking. But as the barge was pushed onward, the clay eroded and the gasoline began to leak out.

In the end, the cost to Graywater for barge repair and environmental penalties was significant; the cost to Frank and Jerry for their violation of the law was much greater. As a result of their failure to report their grounding, they were terminated from employment and lost their US Coast Guard licensing. Frank and Jerry will never be allowed to make the same mistake again.

SAM AND ROY

In defense of Frank and Jerry, they could have cited Graywater's culture as one of the primary reasons they stealthily continued on after the grounding at Forked Island. Both could give testimony that the unwritten directive at Graywater Marine was to keep the vessel moving at all costs. No excuses accepted. The directive had been imprinted on Graywater's personnel by the company's domineering founding father, Sam Arnold.

Like many strong-arm entrepreneurs who passionately feel that their way is the only way, Arnold surrounded himself with yes-men. This was evident in one upper-level manager who, when I asked what value he thought Arnold saw in him, quickly replied, "My obedience."

At the time of the *Fortune*'s grounding, Sam Arnold was no longer Graywater's owner and president; he was reaping the financial benefits of the earlier sale of Graywater to a large conglomerate. But his overriding presence and the culture it had created were still present in Graywater's daily operations, merely transferred to a group of Arnold's handpicked managers who struggled to fill the leadership void created by his departure.

No one struggled more than a key member of Graywater's shore staff, operations manager Roy Harbin. In an interview with me shortly before the *Fortune*'s grounding, Harbin admitted, "I remain perplexed as to why Sam Arnold might have ever chosen me to accomplish some of the duties I was assigned." Even with Arnold gone, he said, "I, to some degree, feel uncomfortable with the duties that I am assigned right now." Despite his confusion, Harbin did not communicate his discomfort to anyone in the company; open and honest communication was not the Graywater way. Unfortunately for Frank and Jerry, Harbin carried the same attitude into his duties as their immediate supervisor. No communication of concerns to Roy was allowed.

Roy Harbin was not the only one frustrated. A hostile work environment among all the managers in Graywater's office had continued for years. Office infighting was so bad that vessel officers felt it better to not bother the office with any communication whatsoever, routine or emergency. They wanted to avoid the risk of being sucked into the affairs of a bickering staff of adult brats whose hostility at times became physical.

Leading the periodic rage was the man most responsible for befriending and helping Graywater's vessel officers, Roy Harbin. In my report on Roy, I stated, "He revealed (to me) that he does have a tendency to repress his feelings and hold them inside, and that from time to time they boil forward and come out in the form of anger or hostility. . . . He loses his temper, but his temper does not last very long."

As Roy's coworker and close friend admitted, "Roy is hard-headed and blows up over the simple things, but our underlying friendship sees it through." Frank and Jerry must not have felt like they were Roy's friends, able to withstand his petulance, because they never picked up their radio to report the grounding of their vessel. In their minds, the directive "keep moving, no excuses" was a better alternative—ethics and values be damned.

A Crisis of Character

You might ask, "Why should the story of Graywater Marine concern us?" Because we all know or can identify a Sam Arnold in today's business world, perhaps from our own workplace. We are also likely to identify a Roy Harbin or a Frank or Jerry. We know these guys or the type of person they represent. What they do to disrupt, weaken, or endanger the workplace is still out there in every business environment. The adult brats of Graywater Marine are no different from any in countless organizations. Character deviance knows no bounds.

In Graywater Marine, we see how deeply adult brats can erode the values that sustain a productive business. What Graywater reveals, and what my work with other businesses confirms, is that adult brats remove from the workplace three cornerstone values that distinguish sound ethical character. These values are honesty, loyalty, and compassion. Later on, we'll stop on our hike down the trail and camp out at each of these "value locations."

The crisis of character started in the mid-1970s when a generation of value-challenged workers entered the American workplace. Now this generation and its successors form more than 75 percent of the American labor force, and they have slowly created work environments that increasingly reflect the behavioral problems of the troubled youth who participated in my wilderness camping trips from 1977 to 1997.

As a result, businesses have begun spending disproportionate time and effort attempting to manage the personal maturity issues—ongoing adolescent-like problems—of their employees, including the absence of values that prevent unethical behaviors. Prior to the mid-1970s, workers seemed to possess these values before they started their careers. After the mid-1970s, the struggle to get workers to do the right thing began in earnest.

From the headlines of today's newscasts, you've probably noticed two drastic effects of the crisis I've described. First are the incredibly irresponsible business decisions that have cost millions of workers their job security and retirement plans, prompting congressional investigation and a monetary "bailout plan" that will potentially cripple future generations. Second are the business ethics violations that have resulted in ethics-controlling legislation, such as the Sarbanes-Oxley Act of 2002 and the Dodd-Frank Act of 2010. But it is in the unpublicized trenches of daily business operations that the crisis is felt the most, taking its greatest toll on the American worker. This is where responsible workers of sound character struggle to cope with the increasing impact of valueless immaturity presented to them by coworkers.

The hardest hit are older line-level supervisors attempting to manage increasingly uncontrollable entry-level workers who view the workplace either as their playground or their temporary stop on the way to corporate glory. George Adams, a hardworking retail warehouse supervisor, painted a realistic picture of the "employee with an attitude" whom he is often forced to "babysit." Speaking of one employee, Adams said to me, "I have constant trouble with him mouthing off in front of customers and getting too close to women customers, as if he's trying to pick them up. He'll also get into verbal arguments with coworkers in front of customers if he even remotely thinks that his judgment is being challenged." The guy sounded like a hormonally hyperactive teenager to me, except he was twenty-eight.

ADOLESCENTS AT WORK

I love how author Rick Jolly captures the immaturity of military personnel in his book *Jackspeak: A Guide to British Naval Slang and Usage*. In the book, Jolly quotes British military officer-fitness reports. See if these excerpts describe the adolescents-at-work syndrome:

- "Since my last report, this officer has reached rock bottom and has started to dig."
- "This young lady has delusions of adequacy."
- "His men would follow him anywhere, but only out of morbid curiosity."

My favorite, though, is "He would be out of his depth in a car park [parking lot] puddle."[2]

Laugh as we might, the reality is that many adult-age workers are growing through their adolescence while at work, right in front of our eyes, and more laborers of similar substance are on the way. This is why businesses are paying increasing attention to the pre-employment screening process in eliminating job applicants who cannot communicate effectively, work in a team, and problem-solve in a positive manner—all value-based skills requiring personal maturity. As one human resources director put it, "My job is to attract, develop, and retain. But attract *what*? It's getting harder and harder to find anyone of character worth attracting."

It's not just the eighteen- or nineteen-year-old, entry-level worker we're talking about. Businesses have become suspicious of the maturity and values of twenty-something employee applicants possessing college degrees, many with sparkling academic records from prestigious universities. The academic résumé no longer has sole priority; now the personal values of the applicant bear equal scrutiny.

To assess the personal values of applicants, more employee recruiters are accessing social networking web sites where applicants may have posted revealing personal information that reflects their values and attitudes—insight not available on a résumé. Increasingly, red flags about an applicant's personal behavior are appearing.

Writing about this trend in the *New York Times*, Alan Finder states that some applicants are discovered to have posted "risqué or teasing photographs and provocative comments about drinking, recreational drug use and sexual exploits in what some mistakenly believe is relative privacy." Mr. Finder concludes, "When viewed by corporate recruiters or admissions officials at graduate and professional schools, such pages can make students look immature and unprofessional, at best."

One university career center director interviewed by Mr. Finder stated, "It's a growing phenomenon." Another stated that businesses were weighing the information found on the applicant's web site against the values of the corporation. She said businesses are asking, "Is there something about their lifestyle that we might find questionable or that we might find goes against the core values of our corporation?"[3] Often the answer is yes.

The crisis of character brought on by immaturity has resulted in a costly lesson that corporate America has learned: putting the power of business into the hands of an emotionally adolescent adult leads to irresponsible behavior, lost profits, lost jobs, and ultimately disgrace. Yet this is an apt description of what businesses have allowed to happen by accommodating emotionally preadult workers at all levels in the workplace. Adult brats are not good for business.

THE SCOPE OF THE PROBLEM

I want to make one thing clear. I'm not saying that all workers entering the workforce for the first time since the mid-1970s are adult brats. But to some managers, it sure seems like it. The safety manager of a defense industry missile production facility recently told me that she had six new workers assigned to her area during the past year. "Only one of the six demonstrates any kind of work ethic at all," she said. "The others act as if they are entitled. They're just along for the ride."

If it had been a cigar-chomping, late-middle-aged macho male telling me this, I'd have been tempted to discount the observation and stash it away in my COF file, where I put Crusty Old Fart remarks. This woman, however, is an early thirty-something professional who was remarking about workers close to her own age.

Five out of six missile-producing defense industry workers with no work ethic. Makes me feel safe; how about you? It's time we faced the truth indicated by the safety manager: there are more adult brats in the workforce than suspected, and the situation is only getting worse.

Even the teaching profession has become stained by the actions of adult brat teachers. Jacquielynn Floyd, a columnist for the *Dallas*

Morning News, captured the essence of this trend when commenting on yet another case of a young female teacher caught having sex with one of her students.

"A common thread some of these cases seem to share is a peculiar reluctance by the perpetrators to grow up," she wrote.

"There's much cultural hand-wringing out there about youngsters who are too eager to behave like teenagers. But at the other end of the conveyor belt are people in their 20s and even their 30s who stubbornly want to pretend that they're still adolescents."[4]

By sheer numbers alone, the workers who bring us the crisis of immaturity are taking over the workplace. An extensive survey on workplace ethics found that 31 percent of US workers have witnessed coworkers engaging in ethical misconduct.[5] Take a deep breath and don't let that statistic vaporize so quickly. This means nearly one-third of American workers, a staggering 48 million people, have witnessed workplace behaviors that should not happen.[6]

The survey is not the only report to indicate the massive extent of the crisis. Every statistical measure of aberrant employee behavior—lying, stealing, harassment—that I have read in preparation for writing this book indicates a steady rise in the frequency of those behaviors over the past decade.

If some argue that a high degree of unethical conduct exists because workers don't know any better, or believe that the line between right and wrong work behavior is indistinguishable, I would have to say they are wrong. Again according to the survey, 78 percent of US workers state that their companies clearly define unethical and ethical behavior to their employees.[7] So it's not a matter of missing knowledge to discern between good and evil. The adult brat, who knows what is right, willingly chooses to do what is wrong.

Another effect of the increased number of adult brats is the growing distrust felt between American workers and their business leaders. This trend is particularly evident when the beliefs of the younger work generation are compared with those of older workers. In a comprehensive Harris Interactive survey, only 36 percent of US workers said they believe their managers act with honesty and integrity. However, workers over age fifty-five were 12 to 14 percent more inclined to trust top management than workers aged eighteen to fifty-four.[8]

I don't want to sound alarmist, merely realist, but the battle line for the productive values of America's labor force has been solidly defined as the younger, more adult-brat-prone workers versus older, more emotionally mature ones. And, because 75 percent of today's workers entered the workforce after 1975, the cards seem stacked in favor of character problems rooted in emotional immaturity.[9]

Let's not forget the members of the younger work generation who transcend adolescence and present themselves as desirably mature workers. There is a healthy, though steadily diminishing, number of them who recognize what is wrong in their workplace and ask challenging questions about how to fix it. (Remember Billy Taylor's concern over his supervisor, Jake, in chapter 1?) They need the assistance of energized older workers to help them overcome the crisis of character fostered by adult brats. What they have no use for is the sour individual who is waiting for retirement, believing the business world is doomed to failure.

First Steps

Like it or not, the American business crisis of character is intertwined with the American crisis of social forces and values. A good friend of mine who is an upper-level manager for a large wireless company put it this way: "Why do you think we outsource so much of our labor overseas? It isn't just to save dollars on pay and benefits. In many cases, foreign workers give us values like honesty and loyalty that we are simply finding harder to identify in Americans."

It hurts to hear frank appraisals like my friend's because it points to a destiny that should scare every American spitless. If current labor trends continue as they are, the United States will soon be unable to rely on its own labor force to provide the price-less values of employee conduct that has made it the premier economic force in the world.

We need to ask, how did we get into this crisis and what can we do to get us out of it? Something has happened in our society to put us in this mess, and we need to clean it up. Otherwise, American business will become grounded in an ethical Forked Island wiggle from which there is no return.

What caused it and what to do about it are questions we answer in the rest of this book. Before we proceed, here are four essential steps you should take first, both personally and in your workplace. Consider these tasks your starter kit for correct thinking.

1. Stop Denying That Anything Is Wrong

I call the attitude of denial the rotten apples attitude. You know, *a few rotten apples spoil the barrel.* The thinking goes this way: a few bad employees are all that's wrong. There is no large-scale problem, only isolated problems tied to certain individuals.

If you hold this theory, stop. You can't excuse well-documented deviant behavioral trends this way. I hit you with a few eye-opening labor statistics earlier, but I omitted mounds of data concluding that most measures of undesirable employee behavior are trending toward the negative—and have been for a long time. You're swimming upstream if you think a few isolated individuals are the cause.

And if you think that your business is immune from the crisis because your corporate values render you adult brat-proof, I hope you are right. But I'm sorry to say that there are few businesses for which this is true.

2. Recognize the Full Scope of the Problem

Business problems and social problems are symbiotic. If adult brats at work are like delinquents, then they reflect the problems of a society that contributes to their delinquency. Your employee problems are directly tied to the society in which the employees live. You can't divorce the two, so you need to look at the problem of adult brat behavior in a holistic light.

While you must deal with employee behavior issues and value decisions on an individual basis, assigning individual responsibility where it belongs, you cannot ignore the larger framework of social causes. You must start giving serious thought to how your workplace environment reacts to the social environment that shapes it.

To blame individual adult brats without identifying and addressing all contributing factors to their delinquency is to consider only part of the problem. The result you will get when you do this is at best a partial solution.

3. Talk Constructively about Solving Adult Brat Problems

I'm not talking about conducting another Salem witch hunt or starting an adult brat-of-the-day watch. Minimally, however, you should know what values your business espouses and begin to talk both formally and conversationally about how those values are currently being evidenced in employee behavior. Don't wait for the employee review process to do this.

If the company mission statement declares that employees will act with honesty in relation to customers, yet you know this is not always the case, then a good question to ask coworkers is "How are we doing in achieving honesty at all times with our customers?" Most of the time, your coworkers know exactly how the corners of customer service are being cut and who is cutting them, but the ostrich-head-in-the-sand strategy reigns in most workplaces. Your goal is to get the ostrich to raise its head and run around a little. Ever see an ostrich run? It's awkward, just like your initial conversation with coworkers might be. But don't get discouraged.

This is only the beginning of how you correct a negative behavioral trend. Take it easy. At this point you are simply opening a dialogue. I'll tell you when it's time to call out the storm troopers.

4. Think of Creative Solutions That Are Personally Challenging

An experienced manager once told me, "Don't worry about rocking the company boat, because it's already sinking." Your work environment may not feel significantly challenged by adult brats—yet. Then again, it may be and you just don't know it.

There is a lot of truth in the words of quality expert W. Edwards Deming, who said profound knowledge must come from outside the company. Sometimes the captain is the last one to know that the boat is sinking.

I encourage you to think critically with those who are outside the influence of your work environment. Harmful behavioral trends are seldom corrected through stodgy, conventional thinking.

What's your creatively radical solution to the crisis of immaturity that's creeping into your workplace? Start thinking about it. I share mine with you later in this book.

For now, take off your backpack, set up camp, and kick back around the campfire. You deserve it. I've already given you your food for the day—that is, food for thought. Now prepare yourself for a scary campfire story full of grotesque characters, because I'm going to tell you what adult brats look like beneath their skin.

Chapter Three

A Dark Heart

To begin the description of workplace adult brats by referencing a juvenile prison environment may seem harsh. Then again, you may share in the sarcasm of one blue-collar company manager who told me, "We get our new workers by backing up our truck to the state juvenile penitentiary."

Don't laugh. America's prison systems have become a prime recruitment ground for blue-collar laborers. One job fair in Des Moines, Iowa, drew recruiters from thirty companies that took applications from three hundred ex-cons and soon-to-be-released prisoners.[1]

Please don't get offended here. I have nothing against the employment of those in the criminal community who are prepared to serve as responsible employees. Twenty years of my life were spent rehabilitating young offenders so that they could do just that. But this is my scary story as we sit around our campfire, and I'll start it where I want. Ready?

Once upon a time (as long as it was 1977), I awakened to the beginning of business adult brathood. It was then that I first saw most of the collective symptoms we now see in jerks on the job. It was my first year conducting wilderness camping trips for juvenile delinquents in the Dallas County (Texas) Juvenile Department prison system. The youths who participated in my rugged expeditions were exposed to character-building opportunities designed to rapidly enhance their maturation process. Looked on then as a last-chance, "tough love" opportunity for incorrigible teens to develop acceptable life values, such programs today are a mainstay in the therapeutic treatment of troubled youth.

To track the results of the expeditions, I assisted a coworker in collecting personality measurements of both our campers and a control group of nontrip participants. Looking back on this research three decades later, I realize that we gathered not only a detailed snapshot of the temperament of a 1970s-era juvenile delinquent (much of which we see in the adult brat sector of today's American workforce) but also clues to how our society opened the door for that disposition to infiltrate our business environment. Following these clues, as we do in the following chapters of this book, leads to specific root causes of the current crisis of personal immaturity and valueless behavior in the workplace. If we know the cause, we can prescribe a remedy to stop it.

Embarking on this trail requires you to fully understand what I mean by juvenile delinquency. So I am providing a snapshot of my delinquents: the skeletal structure of today's adult brats. If you read chapter 2 in this book and could identify in your work experience the problem employees I described there, you'll likely see them somewhere in this grotesque picture, devoid of character.

CLICK

What's your idea of a juvenile delinquent? Mine first formed in the mid-1960s when a group of delinquent girls from a reform school visited my church for a social event. I remember how we gawky teenage boys, wide-eyed over the prospect of socializing with "loose women," entertained the girls in our youth fellowship hall. One girl was particularly chatty as we engaged in a friendly game of billiards. Our conversation turned tantalizing when she suggested we visit her after she was released from confinement. But as I looked at her with my best Romeo stare, I couldn't help noticing the pool cue she held in her hands. Was her return look come-hither, or was the tightly gripped pool cue a message for me to go away? Not wanting to risk injury to body or reputation, I chose to curtail my curiosity.

Any ambiguity I felt then was clarified a decade later when the personality data I collected as part of my wilderness program provided a clear definition of juvenile delinquents. Three characterizations of delinquency stand out in that data, verifying not only why I was wise to walk away from a young girl holding a pool cue but also pointing to what I fear is an increasing descriptor of today's labor force.

"I WILL DESTROY ~~YOU~~ ME"

First, my delinquents possessed abnormal scores in personality traits—nervous, depressive, subjective, and hostile—that resulted in borderline self-destructive behavior.[2]

Not earth-shattering news? I didn't think so either. That's what irresponsible people are, aren't they? They're self-defeating—the type of people your mama told you to stay away from because you risked getting sucked into their impending personal implosion.

That would seem to describe James Pacenza, a former machine operator at an IBM manufacturing plant. Pacenza was fired by IBM "because he visited an Internet chat room for a sexual experience during work after he had been previously warned."[3] The incident resulting in Pacenza's dismissal occurred when a coworker informed IBM authorities that he saw some sexually vulgar chat entries on Pacenza's workstation computer.

The irony is that Pacenza sued IBM for wrongful termination despite admitting he often spent time in adult chat rooms during work hours. A Vietnam War veteran, Pacenza claimed he suffered periodic bouts of depression and anxiety caused by post-traumatic stress disorder. In turn, he said, this caused him to lose behavioral self-control, throwing him into a state of sexual and Internet addiction to escape the horrors of his disorder. He termed his escape "self-medication."[4]

Let's see. He was depressed, nervous, and subjective enough—emotional, illogical, self-absorbed—to render him unable to comply with IBM's written-in-stone Internet use policies. And hostile? He sued IBM for $5 million.

I have great sympathy for the brave soldiers who risked physical and mental injury in the battlefields of Vietnam. But Pacenza has his terms confused. He isn't self-medicating continually because of a four-decades-old war-caused disorder; he's imploding repeatedly because he exercises little self-discipline in following authority, just as juvenile delinquents do when given leeway.

Pacenza's fight against his former employer demonstrates a hallmark of the hostility-driven self-destructive adult brat employee. It is the willingness of the employee to turn annoying passive-aggressive behavior into harmful active-aggressive action.

Typically, miserable employees who exhibit passive aggressiveness will limit their behavior to irritating actions that make others feel miserable, too. It's the self-centered tit-for-tat "misery loves company" ploy, where the objective is to drag others down into a pity party.

In the workplace, I frequently see this behavior exhibited by employees who murmur, meddle, and meander. Let me explain what I mean by those terms:

- *Murmuring*: Talking behind others' backs, creating false rumors, uttering crude, shocking comments, and conspiring against authority figures or the organization they represent.
- *Meddling*: Getting into the "space" of coworkers by acting unofficially on their behalf, misappropriating resources allocated to them, altering their work reports or results.
- *Meandering*: Exhibiting crippling lethargy through the continuous postponement of job duties due to suspect reasons, the use of lame excuses, and wandering from one thing to another while not doing much.

Likely you've seen several of these behaviors in your workplace. They are fairly common irritants. But annoying employees become self-destructive adult brats when they take these behaviors to damaging extremes, resulting in serious damage to others as well as themselves. These actions might include fraud, violence, harassment, and frivolous litigation (like Pacenza's), costing businesses revenue that might otherwise benefit productive employees and investors.

I often witnessed the ease with which troubled kids crossed the line to more aggressive behavior, and one time I actually felt it. It happened when an imprisoned teen who did not want to participate on one of my wilderness trips expressed his protest through every type of passive-aggressive action. He didn't want to go. The authorities relented and excused the young man from my trip. See how far the wrong type of behavior can take you?

But this troubled individual wasn't satisfied with winning the battle through such meager means. He possessed a hostility that pushed him to more demonstratively exhibit his displeasure with my outdoor plans for his life. So when I visited him in the prison's gymnasium shortly after he was excused from my trip, he proceeded to place a jarring roundhouse karate kick in the middle of my back when I wasn't looking. An assault? Yes, one that landed him in isolation—a hellhole far worse than the Colorado wilderness where I had planned to take him.

The adult brat at work is little different from the self-defeating young man who sought to punish both me and himself in the extreme for whatever perverted cause he invented. Can you think of someone who fits this description? I can immediately think of two: towboat captains Frank and Jerry, punishing Graywater Marine for sticking them with adult brat shore supervisors and poor working conditions.

"I REALLY LOVE ME"

Self-defeating behavior is the first characterization I found in my personality profiles of juvenile delinquents. The second is that my delinquents demonstrated a borderline tendency in the area of emotional withdrawal or inhibition. They stuffed their real emotions inside, not showing their true self, fearful of being hurt or rejected by others.[5] Again, doesn't this sound like our towboat captains who crawled inside their emotional shell to avoid conflict?

While my delinquents didn't have the same stress-induced emotional hole exhibited by workers in high-risk occupations, it's close. Nobody should mistake the cool demeanor of an airline pilot who blocks out emotions through "stress inoculation" with the fear of hurt or rejection that causes a delinquent to clam up. But when you are on the receiving end of such emotional freeze-out, who cares about the motive?

Listen to the angst of an oil refinery maintenance worker as he told me about an unwritten code that governs employee interaction in his workplace: "I think there is a code of silence in the field," he said. "One guy told me that he was holding a measurement with a tape and the superintendent kicked the tape out of his hand. I know two persons that quit their job because of the same reason."

Two people quit their jobs instead of voicing displeasure or reporting the supervisor. Why? In large part because they knew that they risked being rejected by coworkers, or physically hurt, if they spoke out. What's the difference between their emotional withdrawal and that of the delinquents who went on my trips?

While the unemotional facade of some of my trip participants made them appear blatantly antisocial, I saw them as patently narcissistic. They sometimes demonstrated extraordinary—if not fake—emotional dexterity, but only to the extent that it suited their extreme selfishness and inflated sense of worth. They were like actors who, in the name of entertainment, conjure undisciplined and insincere emotions to achieve self-serving goals (making the audience laugh and cry) while hiding their genuine personal nature.

Nobody exemplifies this thespian hypocrisy better than actor Matthew Fox of ABC Television's *Lost*. (I'm not being harsh here. The Greek word for *actor* is our modern word *hypocrite*.) On his television program, Fox portrayed a medical doctor who is emotionally stable compared with other cast members, had a pragmatic grasp of life, and possessed a sense of fairness. The off-screen Matthew Fox is a horse of another color, an adult brat whose genuine nature is carefully masked from the viewing audience.

In a brief moment of honesty, here's how Fox described his real self: "I'm a liar and a cheat and a thief and the ultimate manipulator. You can never believe a [expletive] word that comes out of my mouth. I tell lies every day, man. And when I say I'm phenomenally manipulative, I am."[6]

Continuing his confession of grossly immature behavior, Fox admitted getting friends drunk so that they "say and do things they normally wouldn't say or do," intentionally shocking people with his nudity, creating marital disharmony because of his dishonesty, and hiding his true behavior from his kids. In summary, he said, "I really enjoy that process of sort of—well, I [expletive] with people a lot."[7]

Do you hear that? Fox admits to using his ability to mask his true self—his true emotions—as an excuse for behaving selfishly. He's got people fooled. Like my deceptive juvenile delinquents, he's mastered the portrayal of false emotions to achieve goals while masking his true nature.

Business managers tell me this is the most observable trend they see in the so-called Generation Me workers, roughly defined as age eighteen to forty. And despite their self-anointed reputation as a generation driven by emotional honesty, their business reputation is marked by the lack of emotional bonding between themselves and their job, their company, or others on their work team.

Human resource specialists call this bonding factor "employee engagement," defined as the degree to which employees are contributing fully to the success of the organization and find great satisfaction in their work. Recent measurements of employee engagement indicate it is at an all-time low at every level of the business organization, with the lowest rates at the Generation Me level. One study concluded that only 29 percent of workers are fully engaged, while 19 percent are completely disengaged.[8]

Professor Jean Twenge of San Diego State University, a noted generational researcher and member of Generation Me, describes the trend bluntly. "I see no evidence that today's young people feel much attachment to duty or group cohesion," she says. "Instead, young people have been consistently taught to put their own needs first and to focus on feeling good about themselves. This is not an attitude conducive to following social rules or favoring the group's needs over the individual's."[9] Nor does it make for a sincere employee of good character.

"I Gotta Run"

After self-defeating behavior and emotional detachment, the third description of my juvenile delinquents comes from a surprising source: the US Army. During the Vietnam War, shortly before I began my wilderness program, the Army experienced higher than acceptable rates of AWOL (absent without leave) cases. To better identify potential AWOL candidates, the Army's chaplain corps conducted a study of the personality types of recruits and draftees, eventually narrowing the definition of a potential AWOL candidate to an easily recognizable personality profile.[10]

The personality analysis used by the Army is the same one I used to assess the troubled kids on my camping trips, resulting in a ready-made Uncle Sam measuring stick against which I could better predict troublesome runaway candidates. By 1980, after two years of collecting personality data from my campers, I concluded that the average temperament of my delinquents describes a perfect AWOL candidate. Delinquents inherently want to run away from authority and the self-discipline it enforces.

Again you say, not surprising. Don't all troubled kids want to run away from authority? Perhaps. But what should concern you is the result of current profiling I've conducted of employees in various industry sectors using the same personality analysis I relied on for troubled kids. The collective results of those employee profiles indicate the widespread presence of "likely AWOL" syndrome in the American labor force, regardless of authority or rank. Simply put, American business faces an onslaught of employees who, like my delinquents, do not possess the self-discipline to stay the course—to not run away from their job—and who illogically think the grass is always greener on the other side.

This conclusion is echoed in the study of employee engagement cited previously. The study concluded, "There is a strong correlation between engagement and retention."[11] The vast majority of engaged employees exercise the self-discipline to stay with their company; they don't run away. Conversely, those who limit emotional bonding, such as delinquents and Generation Me workers, are prone to go AWOL, leaving their company unexpectedly without explanation or good reason.

I saw this trend overwhelm certain blue-collar industry sectors starting in the mid-1990s. While the technology sector was then fighting its own battle to fill vacant job openings, blue-collar companies were devouring each other in an attempt to lure able-bodied qualified workers away from their current employer. At times, the difference offered in hourly pay was only 25 cents, but it was often enough to entice AWOL-prone laborers to switch employers on the spot. In the rare occurrence when exit interviews were conducted, employees seldom cited increased pay or benefits as a reason for leaving. Instead, it was the perception that they would be treated better when working for "the other guy." The grass was always greener somewhere else.

Such AWOL syndrome/delinquent-like behavior is on the rise in today's workforce. Although it's easy to pick on the egomaniacal rank of professional athletes for an example, the comments of former Major League Baseball player Jason Botts are too appropriate to pass up. Despite great expectations, Botts failed in four attempts provided him by the Texas Rangers baseball organization to play at the major-league level. On learning of his contract release from the Rangers, Botts issued this statement: "I think I've been here for a pretty long time and I deserve a fresh start somewhere else.

I think there's plenty of examples of people leaving the Texas Rangers and going on to really great things. There could be something huge in my future."[12]

Hear that? A false sense of entitlement born of emotional withdrawal from reality and bolstered by a wistful dream of green grass. This is the attitude of many employees of the present, my delinquents of the past.

The Whole Ball of Wax

I hope my snapshot helped clarify what you should look for inside an adult brat. Focus on:

- A self-destructive nature that disregards rules and consequences.
- An emotionally withdrawn temperament wrapped in toxic self-centeredness.
- An AWOL tendency marked by illogical disloyalty.

Knowing the correct indicators of the immature, delinquent-like behavior of adult brats is vital to determining its primary cause. And when you look for this cause, it's important to distinguish the difference between the whimsical, inane antics of the passive-aggressive coworker who simply annoys you—talking too much, showing up late, occasionally shirking duty—and the darkly devious behavior of someone who is self-destructive, emotionally unengaged, and constantly looking to jump off your ship after lighting the fuse that may blow it up.

Signs

If you've paid close enough attention during this ghost story describing an adult brat x-ray, then perhaps you've noticed that there is an easily recognizable behavioral indicator pointing to possible adult brats. It's an indicator or marker I've used several times in our conversation. It's *self-discipline*, or more correctly, the lack of self-discipline.

Makes sense, doesn't it? Ask yourself, what would prevent James Pacenza's repeated implosions? Answer: better self-discipline in following the rules of his company. What would prevent the emotionally withdrawn employee from lapsing into a con-man game of false and manipulative emotive display? More self-discipline, particularly in the exercise of personal honesty. What is required to steer aside the impulse to constantly jump the employment ship? You guessed it.

Self-discipline is essential to helping us comply with the desired standards and values of life. Respected twentieth-century journalist and commentator Walter Lippmann stated that "above all the other necessities of human nature, above the satisfaction of any other need, above hunger, love, pleasure, fame—even life itself—what a man most needs is the conviction that he is contained within the discipline of an ordered existence."[13] If you were to look for one sign that coworkers are mired in adult brathood, fighting against the containment of your company's behavioral standards, look for the self-discipline (or lack thereof) with which they conduct themselves.

Now, ask me how my delinquents scored on the section of the personality assessment that measures self-discipline. I bet you think they scored off the scale, totally undisciplined. But you'd be wrong. Their personality data indicated self-discipline was one of their greatest strengths. Then again, those kids were in prison, a habitat ready-made for cultivating and enforcing the disciplined pursuit of the civilized values of life. Their answers reflected their environment.

Let them get outside that environment, say on one of my camping trips, and they would go totally ape, letting loose all manner of self-destructive behavior. Release them from confinement totally, into the public, and the result of their true undisciplined self is the horrendously high recidivism rates (rate of return involvement with juvenile authority) that we experience today. Put them into the workforce, working alongside borderline adult brat workers who were reared in our unfettered society and whose behavior increasingly reflects theirs, and they see an opportunity to take charge and ruin the very business institutions that provide them sustenance. In short, they become like John Morton, one of my camp participants, whose story illustrates every challenge faced by business when it does not provide adequate structure to keep adult brat behavior in check.

THE MASTERMIND

John Morton's picture hangs on my wall nearly forty years after I first met him, a testament to what he taught me, a rookie therapeutic wilderness camp leader at the time. If he is alive, John is now over fifty years old. If he's active in the workforce and has experienced any degree of success, he may be working as a supervisor, manager, or higher. That, however, would not be the degree of success I projected for John Morton, far from it, because his temperament included every deviance of delinquency that I've described.

John was not your ordinary white kid suburban criminal; he was the mastermind of a bicycle theft ring in a middle-class neighborhood in Dallas—high-class crime for its time. Friendly and innocent looking, John would exhibit that disposition only as long as he thought he could get something from you or hide something from you. Otherwise, he possessed a cold, calculating demeanor and a silver tongue that could exude praise and sarcasm at the same time. He found it easy to manipulate others for his nefarious purposes while lying low to avoid blame.

One night on the camp trail, John's charm failed him and his adult bratlike behavior was exposed. We had canoed on a public lake to an isolated spot that I thought was far enough removed from civilization to discourage any runaway attempt. The lure of cigarette smoke coming from night fishermen more than a half mile away was something I hadn't planned on. In an undisciplined, nicotine-deprived fit (our campers were not allowed to smoke), John convinced several of his campmates to sneak out of camp, steal the canoes, and bum cigarettes from the fishermen.

Stealing aluminum shell canoes is not as easy or as noiseless as stealing bicycles—a factor that I doubt John considered in his rush to satisfy the need of the moment. So the commotion of banging canoes roused me and another trip leader. We then monitored the runaway group's activity from the shoreline, watching every glow from the inhaled cigarettes.

On returning close to shore, John could be heard quieting his fellow conspirators. "*Sssshhh*. Be quiet or we'll wake up the counselors."

They shouldn't have worried. Jumping from behind a bush that hid us, we directed our flashlight beams to the mastermind's face and shouted, "Gotcha."

John's one-word response, with head lowered to his chest, said it all. "Busted." Then a sly grin broke out on his face. In his perverted mind, he was back in the game that quick.

Instead of "Busted," John should have said, "Exposed," for more came to light that night than a simple runaway episode. First, John showed us the susceptibility of like minds to following adult bratlike leaders. Second, John demonstrated how easy it is for self-discipline to be cast aside by the behaviorally weak once they think a structured environment isn't present. Walter Lippmann calls these weak individuals "disordered men," saying, "Because they are deprived of a rational measure upon their desires, they do not conserve their energy but spend it upon unattainable and unsatisfying ends."[14]

John Morton represents the danger every business manager faces from a growing number of disordered adult brats operating outside the bounds of rational measure. They are the ones who, without conscience, show a tendency to self-destruct without caring about consequences. They display an unrepentant emotional callousness that does not hesitate to drag others into the destructive pit with them and a tendency to abandon a healthy institution that encourages productive behavior—all because of a perceived lack of structure enforcing self-discipline. They must be stopped. And if this danger is increasing with Generation Me, we need only look to the Boomer generation that reared them to understand where they learned their craft.

GOTCHA

Federal Judge Amy St. Eve made only one observation as she sat in front of sixty-three-year-old defendant Conrad Black to deliver his sentence to federal prison. "I frankly cannot understand how somebody of your stature—on top of the media empire that you were on top of—could engage in the conduct that you engaged in, and put everything at risk, including your reputation and your integrity." Black, a Chicago-based media mogul who owned several prominent newspapers, managed only a weak expression of "very profound regret" for the financial crime he had committed against his own company's investors.[15]

Black might have said, "Busted," for he and John Morton have much in common.

At one point in his meteoric career, Black was the swashbuckling darling of those that esteem the fiercely independent successful businessperson who would "tell it like it is" and loved to be quoted in high places. The same with Morton, who without provocation would quickly tell you how many kids he had working for him in his bicycle theft ring.

During my camping trip with John, he delighted in sitting around the campfire, entertaining peers with stories about how he had outsmarted the "stupid police." During one such story, I asked him, "If you're so smart and the police are so dumb, how did you get caught?"

The question shut him up because he knew I had the answer. His kid brother had ratted on him.

In Black's case it was his closest associate, F. David Radler, who testified against him in exchange for a plea bargain. It's amazing what the concept of a structured environment—in Radler's case, prison—will do to an adult brat's perspective, even resulting in healthy, self-disciplined behavior. No doubt the disciplined lifestyle that awaited Radler would wipe clean the rose-colored-glass image of his boss. At age fourteen, Black was expelled from his Toronto private school for stealing exams and selling them to classmates. Fifty years later, Black reportedly remained arrogant enough to openly violate a federal judge's prohibition on tampering with evidence.[16]

Black's former head of investor relations and a witness for the prosecution, Paul B. Healy, pointedly observed during Black's trial, "This is not a happy day and I believe all of this could have been avoided if he [Black] had just dropped the arrogance." Wish all you want, but in the absence of self-discipline, Conrad Black could no more control his self-destructive behavior than could John Morton.

In light of such inevitability, the question to ask is, where did this loss of healthy self-discipline, this gravitation to adult brathood, originate? Figure out where it comes from, then we can stop it. Figure it out, and Judge St. Eve will have the answer to why Conrad Black put his integrity at risk for the sake of out-of-control, counterproductive behavior.

Quiz Time

Setting aside for the moment the larger question of why an increasing number of disordered people litter the workplace floor with their uncaring, narcissistic meltdowns, you need to answer three questions. Call this your adult brat ID quiz or "How well did you listen to the scary story?" test.

1. *Is there someone in your workplace who unapologetically bucks authority, rejecting the rules of business operation that everyone else obeys, and who mocks those who comply?*

If so, you just might have an adult brat on your hands. This person might appear to be nothing more than the master of negative watercooler talk, leading other employees in grousing about anything and everything. But I would keep an eye on this person, regardless of job title or position. He could cost you, your coworkers, and your company in more ways than you think. If his behavior concerns you, talk to a coworker, supervisor, or manager you trust. Document any suspicious behavior with specific reference to date, times, and observed behavior.

2. *Is there someone in your workplace who is extremely difficult to figure out and yet constantly demands attention—someone you can't rely on because the person is an emotional enigma?*

If so, you just might have an adult brat on your hands. This person is likely an enigma to others, too. If you can tolerate her self-centeredness, try to befriend her and get a better "read" on her true nature. Don't play Dr. Phil or Oprah. I mean try to develop a genuine friendship. If you feel an emotional resistance to your advances—beyond that normally associated with shy or retiring personalities—note it and then continue to observe how your work team dynamics may be affected by her temperament. Awareness is key.

3. *Is there someone in your workplace who always talks about how others have it better, particularly in other companies, and voices an intention to leave your company's employment because of petty reasons?*

If so, you just might have an adult brat on your hands. This person will typically reveal himself, telling you the exact color, texture, and height of the competition's grass. When such talk becomes pervasive or distracting, quietly inform your boss. Don't argue the merits of your company versus the competition. The AWOL syndrome isn't based in comparative merit; it's a sign of deeper personal issues.

MOVING ON

None of these suggestions can provide a permanent solution for any current or potential adult brat behavior from coworkers. We talk about such solutions later in this book. But your answers to the preceding questions will help you determine the scope of the challenge you face in stopping any crisis of personal immaturity in your work environment.

As we head on down the trail together, our discussion will grow deeper, more substantive. That's how it is on a wilderness expedition. You move past the first "shock and awe" stage of the trip—when your hurting body doesn't allow your brain to think deep thoughts—to a point where intelligent conversation, even with troubled kids, mysteriously appears. Scary stories around the campfire give way to probing questions about life, people, character, and values.

Chapter Four

Why Jerks Exist

I don't know about you, but I love the challenge of playing detective. So I get excited about finding contributing factors to the epidemic of fraud that causes American business to annually lose 5 percent of its yearly revenues. In 2014, this loss was $261,000 per incident. The global loss from business fraud was estimated at $3.7 trillion. Staggering, isn't it? For nonprofit organizations, which account for 11 percent of fraud cases, the median loss is lower— $108,000. Yet this figure has increased by 8 percent since 2010.[1] This horrific squander of charitable gifts and hard-earned business revenue should make us doubly determined to find a cause for such crippling behavior. We have two investigative resources to help us.

CHARACTERISTICS POINT TO CAUSES

The first resource is our knowledge of the culprit's temperament. We know that an adult brat (an adult juvenile delinquent) is a self-destructing, emotionally withdrawn potential runaway (a high personnel turnover risk) who exhibits a gross lack of self-discipline in the absence of a restraining social structure. These woeful characteristics point to several general causes for such business-busting behavior.

Don't lose sight of the irony. We're talking about juvenile delinquents from the last century pointing the way to today's causes of damaging employee behavior. And if you believe my reasoning, then by identifying the social causes of adult brat behavior, you can develop countermeasures that stop its crippling effect on your business. At the very least, you can inoculate your business organization from it. Ideally, you can implement solutions that expose adult brats and remove them altogether from your organization.

As a business owner, manager, or employee, you may not want to stick your nose into the social fabric of the United States to understand what creates the human capital that damages your business. If that describes you, my advice is simple: get over it. Examining sociological forces is what you must do to find effective ways to preserve and prosper your business. An explorer mentality is required, as is the courage that accompanies it.

Our knowledge of the characteristics of adult brats creates a trail to follow. At the end of the trail, you'll find the understanding you seek. While you are exploring, remember that established trails exist for a reason. They are the shortest, easiest, and most proven way to arrive at a destination. Choosing to hike off-trail can be rewarding, but it is almost always more difficult. You can attempt to deal with problem employees in ways other than looking for root causes of their behavior, but why would you if you have a trail that leads you right to them?

I'm reminded of Tom, one of the best wilderness camp counselors I've known. Tom and I led a group of troubled youths up to the Continental Divide trail in the beautiful Weminuche Wilderness Area of southwest Colorado. It was day five of our three-week expedition—roughly where you are now in your hike through this book—and the group was relieved to put the grueling day's ascent behind them. Our goal was to establish camp at a small lake slightly below the trail's elevation, and the teen acting as "leader for the day" carried the map and compass to guide us there.

During break time, Tom walked away from the group to "use the facilities" and then returned excitedly, shouting, "I found the lake!" The rest of us followed him blindly—without consulting the map. Tom proceeded to lead us fifteen hundred feet downhill, following a drainage ditch that masqueraded as a trail. When we arrived at the gorgeous lake Tom had spotted, we rejoiced . . . until we discovered it was the wrong lake. The youngster with the map then led us on the exhausting climb back to the place where we began. Tom? He was assigned to hike in the rear. Bad day, Tom.

In the wilderness, no matter what you see ahead of you, nothing replaces a good guidance system to ensure that you arrive at the correct destination. We know a lot about the general characteristics of a value-challenged employee's behavior, but in our search to find the social cause of it, we need a proven method that will steer us to correct conclusions. I have the perfect guide to get us there.

A Model to Guide Us

Our second resource in the forensic process is the loss causation model famously introduced by the late Frank E. Bird Jr. Don't recognize the name? Neither did I, until Art Rollins called me in 1992 and challenged me to help his trucking company overcome his employees' crisis of personal character. Art's dilemma sent me searching for any assistance to help me understand what causes a loss of character. Bird provided the model to acquire that understanding. The same model is capable of guiding us in our search for the deeper causes of adult brat behavior.

The first thing Bird recommends in his model is to tie any incident of loss to what are called *immediate causes*, defined as substandard acts or conditions.[2] These are the readily observed behaviors of the person involved in the loss, such as the behaviors of delinquency we've already identified. Lack of self-discipline is a generalized substandard act of behavior. Frank Goodwin's failure to report his vessel grounding, Roy Harbin's frequent flares of temper, James Pacenza's attempt to excuse his chronic misuse of Internet access, Conrad Black's arrogant violation of a federal judge's order—all are specific substandard acts of behavior. For the purpose of our discussion, we've hiked past this point of Bird's model. You know what this behavior looks like.

Next, Bird directs us to focus on identifying the *basic or root causes* of a loss. That's the stage we're in right now. To direct us to our discovery of root causes, Bird defines two broad areas to investigate: system factors and personal factors.[3]

Using some interpretive liberty (Bird's model was originally developed for safety analysis), we may define system factors as society's "box" in which we are behaviorally allowed to exist. In this box are the expectations for acceptable and unacceptable social behavior, the permissible and the forbidden. Who builds this box and its guidelines? Society and its organizations do—government, business, technology, education, religion, and family.

Personal factors are the individual qualities we bring to the box. It's how we personally interact with the system of behavioral rules, regulations, and expectations put before us, including how we conform or don't conform to those expectations. Personal factors are visible in the form of the everyday personal choices we make while living in the box society builds for us. These choices include how we establish our family unit, rear our children, exercise our faith, communicate with each other, and behave on the job.

Given these two categories of contributing factors, let's allow Dr. Bird's model to guide us to where the crisis of character in the American workplace begins—its root causes. We'll talk about six system factors now and five personal factors later on.

The Defense System: Feeling a Cold Draft

High on the list of system factors contributing to the building of adult brat workers is the absence of the single largest societal influence for building maturity into adolescents: the military draft.

Listen to what Chief Warrant Officer Robert Rangel, the last Vietnam War-era draftee with uninterrupted military service to retire from the US Army, said about his draft experience: "My grades were not that good, and the lady at the draft board got fed up with me. . . . I had to report or go to jail, because *back then they meant it* [emphasis added]." Then Rangel added, "I got caught."[4]

Do you hear what Rangel said? He was playing the system for all it was worth, trying to stay out of the military draft, but got busted because back in 1967 they meant it. The draft was a milepost to every young man signaling that you had better be responsible in life—in Rangel's case, studying hard in college—or Uncle Sam had a plan to make a responsible lifestyle happen for you. So Rangel gave in and reported for duty.

Did Uncle Sam's plan work? Rangel stayed beyond his two-year obligation because, as he said, "I started enjoying my job and the people I worked with." Hear that? His initial resistance to being a member of Uncle Sam's team melted as he learned valuable principles of duty and comradeship—values every business wants its employees to embrace.

On retirement, after forty years of service, Rangel had this to add: "The best thing about being in the military is knowing I come from a very honorable institution of the friendships I have made all the years in the line unit. You grow up as a unit and as a family. I am really going to miss it."[5] You can envision businesses lining up to hire this guy, can't you?

Testimony to the military's power to rapidly mature irresponsible young people continues, but not on the wide, society-changing scale once displayed. Today, the military grants an increasing number of special waivers to allow enlistment of recruits whose blemished behavioral records would otherwise disqualify them from enlistment. Why? Because even though they tend to go AWOL and face court-martial more than other recruits, they also tend to be more loyal to the military in the long term, staying longer and reenlisting at higher rates.[6] In other words, they become like Rangel, maturing because Uncle Sam forces them to.

But it's not just those in need of severe behavioral adjustment whom the military benefits. In 2007, Josh Daniel forestalled his college plans and surprised his parents by joining the military on graduation from high school. Typical of Generation Y, who pride themselves on their engagement in socially responsible causes, Josh said he joined because he felt that helping out people in Iraq "is something I can do. I also wanted self-improvement." Despite his exemplary academic achievements and rock-solid upbringing, he needed emotional maturing.

During his basic training, Josh's noble pursuit was often derailed by fellow recruits of questionable character who had been given the option of "either go in the Army or go to jail." Daniel quickly grew tired of the punishment his training unit received because of the antics of these characters. When I asked Josh if he ever saw a change for the better—over the long haul—in the troubled recruits, his reply was emphatic: "Absolutely." Then he quickly added, "And in me, too, because of them."[7] No doubt Robert Rangel would agree. The military has a way of maturing even the most resistant individual.

Where is this widespread positive social force when so many adolescent-like young men and women need it? In the absence of the systematic military draft, the responsibility for generating this influence has been handed to business.

The Government System: ## Of, By, and For Adult Brats?

Sadly, it can be argued that the increase in troublesome employee behavior reflects a government that lately has grown more deficient in character and wisdom. Those seeking excuses for improper behavior need only look to the growing disassociation of our laws, lawmakers, and law enforcers from the values of self-discipline and accountability. After all, why exercise prudence in obedience to the laws of our society when the organizations and individuals responsible for those laws aren't deemed worthy of following?

Given such a ubiquitous social force as disrespected government, the value-challenged individual feels justified in doing what is permitted by ineffective law rather than what is prudent by sound wisdom. When adult brats' behavior is challenged, their response most often is "I'm only doing what is permitted by authority." Too often, they are correct. In the workplace, irresponsible employees know the letter of the law and its moral intent better than you or I do. They will fight to defend their counterproductive behavior by using every vague letter of poorly created workplace law or policy. When investigated for obstructing justice to cover up the use of his office to gain sexual favors, Bill Clinton argued over the nuances of the definition of sexual harassment—parsing the definition of sex into minutiae, as if one definition of sex in the workplace is permissible while another is not.

If you have trouble believing that our system of government acts as an enabler of those in the workplace who lack personal character, then listen to the words of one former Cabinet leader as he blames our government for the moral trap that caused one of the most pressing business problems of our time: the financial industry crisis in the United States.

During the last years of President George W. Bush's administration, before the financial crisis of late 2008, Treasury Secretary Henry M. Paulson was tasked with developing a blueprint for regulatory reform of the financial industry. Paulson—a man of respected character who had (until the fall 2008 financial crisis) enjoyed bipartisan political support—released his department's study in March 2008. The study's executive summary contains an eye-opening admission of government responsibility for creating the opportunity for immoral behavior in the financial market, stating, "Explicit government guarantees often erode marketplace discipline, creating the potential for moral hazard and a clear need for prudential regulation."[8] In other words, our government, acting through legislators who failed to recognize (or ignored) ethical hazards, created an ineffective regulatory framework that invited those with questionable character to leap into a moral hole.

Given the example of such a government-created opportunity to exercise undisciplined self-destructive behavior, is it any wonder that adolescents grow into adults who believe that our government invites them to cheat the system?

The government also enables the creation of adult brats through well-intentioned yet shortsighted policies designed to remedy social ills and inequality. Think of it as social engineering gone awry. Such was the case in 2006, when the state of New Jersey enacted legislation establishing the highest age limit at which children can piggyback on their parents' insurance policy. The limit set by New Jersey? Age thirty years.[9] Then under the Affordable Care Act of 2010, Congress established the national limit at age twenty-six.

I understand the compassionate reasoning behind the legislation. Good-hearted politicians think insurance is too expensive for young adults starting out in life, so they devised a plan to let the offspring ride longer on their parents' policy.

But such legislation strengthens one of the most powerful social forces creating adult brats: the prolonged adolescence syndrome—the "I don't have to grow up until I'm in my late twenties" disorder. Thanks to the federal government, young adults can still be covered by their parents' health insurance policy while they use their twenty-something years to look for personal fulfillment and find meaning to life. As comedian Yakov Smirnoff famously exclaims about America, "What a country!"

Another social engineering measure that promotes irresponsible adult behavior is state government lotteries designed to boost revenue for education. These lotteries, sometimes called a tax on stupidity, wreak a moral and financial toll on those least able to afford it. A lottery's success is based on people exercising the same lack of self-discipline that characterizes juvenile delinquents. As David Brooks notes, "Here is the government, guardian of order, telling people that they don't have to work to build for the future. They can strike it rich for nothing."[10] Nothing, that is, except the exchange of personal maturity for delinquent folly.

The Education System: I Am the Greatest

Another factor to examine on our hike through the root causes of adult brat behavior is a touchy one: our educational system. I'm not out to denigrate the well-meaning efforts of schoolteachers who labor long and hard to educate our young. Rather, it's the educational system under which they labor that produces an increasing number of high school graduates—future employees—with less than desirable character.

One of the reasons for a decline in the personal values of employable graduates is the system of dishonest self-appraisal taught to students. This system began in earnest in the 1970s when schools began appraising students more on building their self-esteem than on rewarding academic performance. The result is subsequent generations of graduates who have entered the workforce with an unrealistic, inflated sense of self-worth and importance. Senior technical managers like a friend of mine at Raytheon remark that it isn't unusual for new-hire technicians to work for six months, receive only average job performance appraisals, yet think they are entitled to a substantial promotion.

Educational experts call the practice of false self-esteem building "unconditional validation," meaning "feeling good about yourself no matter how you act or whether you learn anything or not."[11] Few know about the widespread use of this practice better than Professor Jean M. Twenge of San Diego State University, who writes, "60 percent of teachers and 69 percent of school counselors agree that self-esteem should be raised by providing more unconditional validation of students based on who they are rather than how they perform or behave."[12]

A veteran second-grade teacher in Tennessee summarized the delusion, saying, "We handle children much more delicately. They feel good about themselves for no reason. We've given them this cotton-candy sense of self with no basis in reality."[13]

When this educationally produced self-worth fantasy meets performance-based job reality, it can quickly lead the disillusioned employee to adopt self-destructive behaviors such as tantrums, the issuance of excessive job demands based on an unrealistic feeling of self-importance, passive-aggressive behaviors, and the beginning of the self-defeating AWOL syndrome of disloyalty. One twenty-three-year-old worker, disheartened when he wasn't considered by his bosses to be as important on his job as he expected, started a blog dispensing advice to others with similar experiences. Listen to his bitterness: "Keep your resume in the flow and continue to network; screw face time—if you've put in your eight hours and accomplished nothing, don't continue to waste your precious time."[14]

Typically, this egocentric pattern begins to appear in a student's high school years when cumulative ego stroking by school officials produces assertive, sometimes arrogant students. In the old days, we'd simply say the student was "feeling his wild oats" and dismiss any acting out as temporary hormonal insanity. But more often, the school system is feeling the bite of the empowered animal it has bred.

Such was the case when a seventeen-year-old high school student from Fairfax, Virginia, called a school administrator at his home phone number to complain about the nonpostponement of school for a snow day. The honor roll student—in a huff because he couldn't locate the administrator in his office—attempted to reach the administrator at his listed home phone number. This prompted a return call from the official's wife, telling the student bluntly what she felt about his breach of civility. I believe the exact words spoken to the young man by Mrs. Administrator were "Get over it, kid, and go to school!" Somewhere in the diatribe she also called him a "snotty-nosed little brat."[15] A bit over the top, if you ask me, but my kind of woman.

The reason we know the wife's exact words is because the student recorded her harangue and his friend posted it on Facebook and YouTube. When questioned about his brash behavior, the student said that "he tried unsuccessfully to contact [the school official] at work and that he thought he had a basic right to petition a public official for more information about a decision that affected him and his classmates. He said he was exercising freedom of speech in posting a Facebook page. The differing interpretations of his actions probably stem from 'a generation gap.' "

Let me correct this misguided adult brat-in-the-making. Your arrogance doesn't stem from a generation gap or freedom of speech issue. It comes from years of coddling by a school system that tells you to feel good about yourself no matter how rude or self-centered you act.

The overwhelming response to the student's story in the comment section of the *Washington Post* is best summarized by this letter from an anonymous reader:

> You know, I wasn't surprised by the student's sense of entitlement in making the call to a home number about a trivial issue. We encourage children to think that they are the center of the universe and that their opinions and desires are more important than those of anyone else, especially those of adults in a position of authority.
>
> If I were on the admissions staff of a college, I would not be inclined to let this kid anywhere within cell phone range for fear of his trying to reach me "at all times." Ditto if I were his college instructor or his future employer.[16]

Do you hear what the reader is saying? Who ultimately pays for the failings of the primary and secondary education system? Businesses, that's who.

To be fair, other practices of the educational system are equally culpable in the production of employees of questionable character. Grade inflation for the purpose of satisfying administrative goals is one, as is the peer pressure on teachers—much of it coming from their organizational hierarchy—to conform to feel-good educational programs that promote symbolism over substance.

I feel for teachers who are told they must not upset the educational applecart that provides the illusion of student greatness, even if the cart is broken. For teachers, the choice is simple: they are to lie low and conform. Why fix the system that creates adult brats when employers can pay for it later?

The Communication System: Can You Feel Me Now?

"Screw face time." Remember these words of advice quoted earlier from the disillusioned twenty-three-year-old who felt his bosses didn't cater to his sense of self-importance? Did you wonder, as I did, why the young man was so quick to suggest giving up personal face-to-face communication time with his supervisors? Or why he considers his other time investments more important than a face-to-face approach to relationship building?

As with many members of his generation, perhaps the skill was never his strength. Reared in an era of easy access remote communication capability, when the boundaries and benefits of systemic faceless communication are still unknown, the need to exercise relationship-building skills—long a requirement in the workplace—may have never crossed his mind.

In the end, when faced with a personal growth opportunity at work, the disgruntled youngster did what our high-tech communication system allows him to easily do. Hang up. Unfriend. Avoid intimacy. End any further investment in emotional dialogue. Run away from the situation. Use an impersonal social networking or commentary Internet site to grouse, while immersing himself in a sea of narcissistic self-pity offered by sympathetic network "friends," few of whom he could pick out in a crowd. He behaved like one of my delinquents, creating a charade of emotional caring to hide his emotional immaturity.

As much as communication systems based on the Internet and wireless technology have allowed us to build a world society accustomed to the benefit of unlimited instant communication, they have also unleashed a social force that encourages its users to practice deceptive or deviant adult bratlike behaviors.

Emotional masking or distancing—the hiding of one's true emotional nature—is the most perpetrated behavior prompted by today's high-tech communication system. It's also one of the three distinguishing behaviors of juvenile delinquents and their workplace counterparts.

When author Betsy Israel solicited input from teens on the implication of their 24/7 use of social networking tools, one seventeen-year-old readily confessed, "There's the issue of removal. Online engagement is not a viable substitute for an in-person social life." Another teen, attempting to put a positive spin on her ample use of instant messaging, said, "You can talk to them [friends] without the problem of facial expressions."[17]

Problem? Only if you are self-centered and insecure, like the twenty-three-year-old who withdrew from interaction with his coworkers because they wouldn't play according to his rules.

Continuing to describe the benefits of messaging, the teen said, "It's controllable; you have time to craft an answer, even if that has a kind of questionable aspect, like you're changing your personality and then when you see that person, uh, it's obvious you've been trying to impress them."[18] Tell the truth, young deceiver. It's embarrassing when you see someone face-to-face for the first time, and it's obvious you lied to them via instant messaging.

This type of self-excusable license to misrepresent oneself, made convenient by our modern communication system, easily leads the perpetrator into another one of the behavioral patterns common to delinquency: self-destruction. This is because self-destructive behavior is the natural by-product of an all-too-easily spun web of deceit that is designed to trick the "listener" but that instead ensnares the sender. Several headline-grabbing instances point to the inevitability of this outcome, but one stands out.

Lori Drew, then forty-seven, of Dardenne Prairie, Missouri, decided to seek revenge on a thirteen-year-old former girlfriend of her daughter, blaming her daughter's emotional angst on the girl, Megan Meier. Drew assumed the false identity of a sixteen-year-old boy and approached Meier on her MySpace social networking site. For weeks, the "boy" cultivated an online love relationship with the girl but then suddenly turned cruel in his comments to her. His final comment to her was "The world would be a better place without you."[19]

Meier, who suffered from mental health problems, promptly hung herself in her closet.

On investigation into Meier's death, Drew's involvement was discovered. Her initial defense consisted of claims that she manufactured the ruse as a concerned parent, simply attempting to find out what happened to make her daughter sad. But the ploy she used, enabled by the ease of our communication system to mask emotional deception, only led her into a natural web of self-destructive behavior that she could have never imagined. By her unprecedented actions, which resulted in her conviction on three misdemeanor counts of gaining unauthorized access to MySpace for the purpose of obtaining information on Meier, Drew set off a storm of legal issues about Internet use that may take decades to solve.

Other incidents highlighting the disparity between our high-tech communication capabilities and its vulnerability to improper use continue to unfold on a daily basis. In Florida, a cheerleader who posted provocative statements about her friends through text messaging and on her social networking site was assaulted by them. The beating was videotaped for posting on the Internet by her "friends" to embarrass her.

In rural Utah, school officials were shocked to discover middle school students "sexting" by sending nude photos to each other via their cell phones. The purpose of the pictures was to solicit dates—a new form of predating ritual. Little thought seemed to be given by the teens as to what could happen to the pictures after they were sent or whether the photos represented child pornography. Psychologists following similar cases blame technology for multiplying the potential for mischief.

It's important to recognize the effect on the workplace of such growing trends. The formative process of creating adult brats grows exponentially and affects our population at an earlier age as technology advances, particularly when it is unleashed without regard to social ramifications.

We have only a vague understanding of what journalism professor Michael Bugeja of Iowa State University calls "interpersonal intelligence"—the knowledge of when, where, and for what purpose technology is most appropriate.[20] What we do know is that with unchecked use of communication technology comes the enablement of behavioral trends closely resembling those of delinquents. If you haven't witnessed it already, perhaps the result of this trend will show up in your workplace in the form of some misfit who makes your employer pay for poor behavioral habits learned from communication devices.

THE COMMERCE SYSTEM: EMPLOYEES GONE WILD

Remember the good old days when the boss was boss? Employees were expected to obey their supervisor, who always had the best interest of his employees at heart. And an unwritten sign existed at the workplace door proclaiming, No Jerks Allowed. Stop laughing. I mean it. This is *my* fantasy. If I want to hearken back to the days of black-and-white television, consider all moms to be June Cleaver, and think of Mr. Dithers (Bumstead's boss) as a considerate employer, humor me.

Or perhaps you're more like me than you think, particularly if you get satisfaction from what veteran pitcher Kevin Millwood did to rookie pitcher Eric Hurley. As a new member of the Texas Rangers baseball club, Hurley was scheduled to accompany Millwood and his team on a visit to the White House, including a personal introduction to the president.

At the last minute, Hurley boarded the team bus destined for the White House dressed in blue jeans and a T-shirt. Millwood tactfully informed Hurley, "No, that ain't gonna work," and sent him back to his hotel room to change into more respectful attire. When Hurley did not return in a timely manner, the bus departed for the White House without him.[21] An experience of a lifetime was lost.

Does this seem cruel to you? Not if you're attempting to achieve the highest level of business teamwork (professional baseball is a business), which produces the greatest possible degree of results when significant amounts of money are at stake, especially when the task involves extruding responsible action from those inclined to callow behavior.

Old-timers might pat Millwood on the back, but what he did is an exception in today's business world rather than the rule. Such values-based leadership is directly opposed by a convoluted system of employee management that often exalts the individual right of the employee over the larger value-based culture of the company. The result is that time-proven management mantras such as "There is no 'i' in team" are no longer effectively true.

Jennifer Cohen is a good example. When an older colleague in her marketing firm told twenty-four-year-old Cohen she was abusing her company's policy on casual dress by dressing too informally, she lashed out in defiance. "Each generation seems to have a different idea of what is acceptable in the workplace, and in this situation I was highly offended. People my age are taught to express themselves, and saying something negative about someone's fashion is saying something negative about them," she said.[22]

Where have we heard this kind of argument before? That's right—it was the defective reasoning of the Fairfax, Virginia, high school student who cited generational differences as the reason it was acceptable for him to call the home telephone of a school official and voice his complaint to the official's wife.

But if the student's faux pas was simply the result of generational impulsive thinking that merely violated school rules (he was disciplined for using his cell phone on the school campus), Cohen's admittedly persistent pushing of the envelope represents something far more significant. In her ultimately successful pursuit of self-expression, she personifies the freedom provided today's employees to place personal goals and values over those established by the employer. And while her motives may be innocuous, the authority-bending success of employees like her has created a perfect breeding ground for problematic employees whose motives are not. These employees are all too willing to ride the coattail of Cohen's brash behavioral groundbreaking, secure in the knowledge that beleaguered managers will give in to each challenge. No wonder they feel free to ply their havoc on the organization. It no longer has the fortitude to try to stop them.

At the heart of this disturbing trend lies a sea of change in the public's perception of business and its upper management ranks, particularly big business. Business is no longer the good guy it was once thought to be. And while it is totally understandable why the reputation of business has suffered from the high-profile self-inflicted corporate wounds of "bad boys" like Countrywide and Fannie Mae, even perennial good guys like Southwest Airlines and Whole Foods have now been tainted with scandal. This is to say nothing about how businesspeople are portrayed in the media, turning the tide of public opinion against the good intentions of business.

One study by Business & Media Institute concludes that businesspeople are most often portrayed on television as "a greater threat than the mob." (You would think it was the mob Jennifer Cohen was up against, judging by her reaction.) During two rating periods, the institute observed thirty-nine prime-time television episodes featuring business plots, noting that 77 percent portrayed a negative view of business and businesspeople.

Commenting on the trend revealed by the study, columnist Clarence Page—no apologist for business—stated that "the study tends to confirm what the institute has long maintained is Hollywood's bias against one of America's most maligned and misunderstood minority groups: business folks." It's no wonder. In the thirty-nine television episodes, Page notes that "businessmen turned up as kidnappers and murderers 21 times, almost as often as the 23 times put together by drug dealers, child molesters, serial killers, and other hardened criminals."[23]

Given the media's powerful ability to shape the minds of young people, the study's author, Dan Gainor, reaches a dark yet realistic conclusion. Given time, he says, "[O]ur children will think you have to lie, cheat or murder to get ahead."[24]

I have news. That time is now.

Our system of commerce, weakened by overly lenient employee management and crippling public perception, no longer provides the structured, authoritative environment that holds in check the behavior of those who abuse their employer to get their own way. Sadly, it enables it.

THE POSTNUCLEAR FAMILY SYSTEM: SPLITTING THE PARENTING ATOM

The most influential of all the system factors contributing to the rise of delinquent adults is the decline of the married, two-parent family unit, the traditional system of parenting. If we compared all the system factors to mountains, the importance of the family unit in preventing or creating adult brats would stand out as Mount Everest.

If you are a single or cohabiting parent, don't hang up on me at this point. I promise not to beat the traditional marriage drum too loudly. But we need to examine some valid points about the relationship of behavioral problems in kids (read: high-risk potential for ending up as troublesome workers) and our marital choices.

First, parenting is the ultimate influence on the outward character of children, and that influence is evident in the workplace. How children witness their parents interact in a significant relationship with each other and with extended family and friends is particularly influential. As a rule, the better a parent models how to build responsible relationships with others, the more likely children are to develop into responsible adults (employees). Admit it: you've sized up an adult brat or two in your years of work experience and wondered, *Gee, did his parents not show him any better?* So have I.

Earlier, I mentioned a public relations firm in Dallas, SPM Communications, that espouses a "jerk-free environment." I asked the firm's owner, Suzanne Miller, where she learned the values that drive her decision to shape her company culture concerning jerks. She said, "I learned those values from my parents." Her dad inspired her "by his unwavering show of support, his strength, his commitment to see a problem through, and his unconditional love. He always told me I could achieve anything I put my mind to. I was fearless in his image, because he believed I could." As for her mother, Suzanne said, "My mom lights up a room. She likes to find the good in every person she meets."[25] Parents, more than any other factor, determine the character of America's workers.

Second, children living in single-, cohabited-, and nontraditional-parent families develop behavioral problems at a far greater rate than those living in married parent families. Sorry. I know this may hurt, but it's true.

According to the Urban Institute, a "considerable volume of research" confirms that children living with single or cohabiting parents are "more likely to be poor, food insecure, read too infrequently, and exhibit behavioral problems than children living with married couples." When cohabitation involves a mother living with a boyfriend who is not the biological father of her child, the likelihood of the child's emotional and behavioral problems increases.[26] I'm willing to wager that many of their problems resemble those of my delinquents of the 1970s:

- Self-destructive behaviors because no one has shown them a healthy path to self-fulfillment.
- Emotional withdrawal and masking because the pain from a barrage of temporary relationships is too great to handle.
- A desire to run away from life's challenges because the fanciful promise of more emotional stability elsewhere is greater than present reality.

The hard fact is that each year close to 40 percent of all newborns—approximately 1.5 million infants—are born to either single or cohabiting parents. If you project this birth rate and marital status over the next twenty years, it amounts to 30 million potential workers entering our labor force by 2030, each of whom is at greater risk of bringing behavioral problems to work than same-age coworkers reared in married-parent families. This is based on Urban Institute research indicating that 15.7 percent of children living in cohabiting families and 9 percent of those in single-parent families will experience emotional or behavioral problems. Compare this with only 3.5 percent of kids living with married parents.[27] Statistically, that's a huge difference. If you are an employer, which group would you want to target as your future employees?

Last, the Pew Research Center has determined that a significant but shrinking percentage of our society (69 percent) believes that it is best to rear children in a household with married parents, yet the number of births to singles or cohabiting individuals is steadily increasing.[28] This dichotomy is directly attributable to two generationally associated social trends that should concern any business interested in securing a viable future workforce.

The first is the sharp decline in value that parents give children. In 1990, 65 percent of adults indicated that children were important to a good marriage. Now that figure has dropped to 41 percent. What factors have replaced children as keys to good marriage? A happy sexual relationship (70 percent), the sharing of household chores (62 percent), adequate income (53 percent), and good housing (51 percent).[29] Thankfully, marital faithfulness (93 percent) ranks highest in importance or else children might end up in single or cohabiting households at an even greater rate. Simply put, our younger generation of parents places less value on children for marital success, replacing them with more self-fulfilling pursuits.

Perhaps this alarming trend is best explained by a second inclination of the younger generation revealed by Pew's research. They attach far less moral stigma to out-of-wedlock births and cohabitation than do their elders. In fact, Pew concludes, "They engage in these behaviors at rates unprecedented in U.S. history." Oblivious to the potential emotional and behavioral ramifications to children born under such circumstances, nearly half (47 percent) of Generation X has spent some time in their life in a cohabiting relationship.[30]

Why there is a decline in moral concern about the change in our social family system is a book unto itself. For business and its tango with undesired employee character, the implications are clear. As the parenting atom proverbially splits, its cost to business increases.

AWE AND SHOCK

If your journey through this book were compared with one of my wilderness trips in the Rocky Mountains, you would now be at the point where you round a bend in the trail or crest the top of a hill, only to stop dead in your tracks. Before you rises a wall of mountains, magnificent in grandeur, frightening in scope. Your first reaction is awe coupled with the inclination to stop and soak up the beauty. Soon shock sets in as you realize that your objective lies on the other side of the wall; there is no way around it. Then doubts about your strength and character begin to form as you consider the task ahead of you. *Can I do this? Do I want to do this?*

You're not alone. When Meriwether Lewis and William Clark set out on their momentous expedition to explore the reaches of the Louisiana Purchase, they knew little about the formidable Rocky Mountains. Lewis recorded his wonder at first seeing the Rockies: "These points of the Rocky Mountains were covered with snow and the sun shone on it in such a manner as to give me the most plain and satisfactory view," he wrote. Then doubts overcame him: "When I reflected on the difficulties which this snowy barrier would most probably throw in my way to the Pacific, and the sufferings and hardships of myself and party in them, it in some measure counterbalanced the joy I had felt in the first moments in which I gazed on them."[31] Sounds to me as if Lewis felt a lump in his throat.

We're at what I call the "swallow hard" spot in our journey toward understanding where adult brats come from and how to defeat them in your workplace. Each of the system factors we've discovered in this chapter is an imposing mountain range unto itself, and all of them work together to create the crisis of personal character that hounds businesses.

- A military system that no longer provides a widespread maturation process for nearly every young man of service age.
- A governmental system that all too often models the wrong behavior and enables us to do the same at work.
- An education system that promotes an antiproductive, self-centered form of performance appraisal.
- A communication system that promises easy interpersonal relationships but results in cold, impersonal, and harmful behavior.
- A commerce system in which well-intentioned employee management has disabled the enforcement of employee maturity.
- A family system trending toward an unhealthy form of parenting that increases the likelihood of producing troubled children, our future employees.

Collectively, these factors are the high mountain range standing in the way of reaching solutions to deep-seated, socially caused business problems. As harmful as they may be in producing desired employees, they also form a collective clue to the few simple things that business can do to stop its crisis of personal character.

Before we can explore those simple solutions, we must examine how the hideous force created by these system factors influences us to act in counterproductive ways to stop the development of troubled employees. We must look at the personal factors of loss causation that act hand-in-hand with the system factors to create a social culture that encourages jerks on the job.

My advice is to set aside your eagerness to charge ahead and tackle the mountain range without proper preparation. When facing such a steep climb, it's wise to first set up a base camp, rest awhile, and prepare for the intense personal scrutiny that lies ahead.

Chapter Five

Encouraging the Jerk Mentality

Each of us can choose how we interact and react to the collective character-busting strength of the system factors described in the preceding chapter. Our reactions, both individually and as a society, are largely determined by what Frank Bird Jr. (see chapter 4) calls our *personal factors* of loss causation, particularly the influence that family, friends, culture, and faith have on our personal values. Personal factors are evidenced by the life choices we make when faced by the system factors that would lead us into adult brathood.

In his book *That Hideous Strength*,[1] C. S. Lewis deftly portrays the role that personal factors play in the struggle to stay the right course against a systemic evil. Lewis weaves a frightening tale of a postwar England where the assault on the free nature of man turns from the external threat of Nazism to the hidden, darker peril of what we, the good people, can do to ourselves. Lewis conjures a small university town in which a stealthy evil academic organization called NICE (National Institute for Coordinated Experiments), attempts to assimilate everyone into its Stepfordlike mindless evil force. This force is dedicated to destroying the noble nature of man.

Gosh, I didn't know Lewis knew my college history professor.

One C. S. Lewis commentator describes the book as "Lewis's dystopian examination of how without firing a shot, the alliance of government, business, academia, and mass media can produce a pure evil of wholesale fascism, all in the name of mankind."[2]

He could have been describing the unified strength of the outwardly benign system factors we've examined, all of which represent supposedly healthy, empowering segments of American society. Their weaknesses, however, can work collectively as a hideous strength propagating widespread behavioral immaturity, particularly in the lives of those whose personal factors (character) are lacking.

I told you that I'm an optimist, although by now you probably disagree. Truly, I would like to think that the noble nature of man can recognize and repel the combined social flaws that have led to the crisis of character in our workplace. But there is strong evidence that the hideous strength of our system factors, like Lewis's NICE, continually overwhelms the best of personal factors and influences people to eschew responsible behavior. I know this personally. Such influence once snared me years ago when I let the hideous strength turn me into a jerk on the job.

The Master of My Mind

Without sounding too metaphysical, my first inclination to surrender any semblance of personal maturity to the hideous strength occurred when I first met John Morton, the juvenile delinquent mastermind from the wilderness trip I described in chapter 3. John is the product of several of the system factors that produce personal immaturity: lack of any forced maturation process, fractured family unit, well-meaning but counterproductive government programs, and a lenient education system.

Emboldened by the collective strength these factors afforded him, John set about to influence my leadership of his camp group. His intention was clear. He not only wanted to negate any positive influence I represented; he wanted to drag me into his pitiful world of jerkish behavioral abnormality. Remind you of any employees you've known? Thought so.

From the moment our group departed on our trip, John used every trick the system had taught him, trying to force me to step out of character. In addition to flaunting an independent, self-centered attitude, he successfully marshaled the strength of his campmates to rattle me. I was subjected to taunts, threats, verbal jousting, acts of defiance—anything to fight back against my mission of helping him to mature. Within the first few days of our trip, Morton had me on my heels, shaken. Worse, he succeeded in driving a wedge between me and the other counselor on the trip. Feeling isolated, I became a jerk in waiting.

In my naïveté, I underestimated the power of the dreadful force that creates people like John Morton. The strength of a wilderness camp counselor lies in the ability to place a camper in a teachable moment, with the opportunity to impart character lessons. With John, the roles were reversed. I was the one being manipulated, not he, as I fought against influencing factors I couldn't control.

When my coworker and I unwisely decided to split our group, each taking half the kids on an overnight group excursion by ourselves, John sensed his opportunity to bring me fully under his influence. He was assigned to my group, and as we hiked down the trail, away from any support I could receive from my coworker, John proceeded to unite his campmates in an all-out assault on whatever remained of my resistance. By nightfall, camped along a small creek in an Arkansas wilderness area, I was toast.

The crowning incident began with a snake. No biblical joke here. I'm like Indiana Jones—I hate snakes. Morton knew this because it was the wedge he used to divide me and my snake-loving coworker.

Finding a poisonous water moccasin along the creek bank, John rallied the group to chase and kill it. Despite my orders to stop the pursuit, John and his buddies continued. When I became more remonstrative, John turned his attack on me, taunting me and threatening to throw a snake under my tarp that night. (Tents? Who needs tents? We are the wilderness camp counselors. We don't need no stinkin' tents.)

The last threat lit my fire, propelling me to the dark side. With volcanic force, I regurgitated all my pent-up feelings in front of the group as I confronted Mr. Morton nose to nose. Drill sergeants and baseball umpires would blush at what I told him. I even surprised myself with a few choice combinations of swearwords.

And what effect did my tirade have on young Morton? He smiled, a sickeningly sweet, sarcastic "gotcha" smile. His mission was accomplished. The hideous strength he represented had won, and for the moment I was an immature, undisciplined jerk on the job, no different from the adult brat he would grow into.

With this story, you now know some of my personal factors. I best resist character compromise when I am in the company of others, such as my camp coworkers, who are doing the same. Separate me from that support line, and I am weakened. Too often, I let the hideous strength influence me.

You have your own personal factors that dictate how you react to the influence of our social system factors. Your challenges differ from mine.

Perhaps your test is maintaining your character in a small company devoid of effective human resource management, the type of work environment where adult brats feel free to wreak havoc because employee management policies are missing. Or it could be in your home life where you struggle as a parent to balance work and child rearing, wanting to model the right character to your child.

One thing you can't deny is that you must navigate a force field of system factors seeking to influence how you responsibly fulfill your general duties in life and your specific duties to your employer. We know what factors combine to create this force. We've examined how the hideous strength creates adult brats. Now it's time to examine how our society as a whole—our collective personal factors—is influenced by it. If you or your business wants to guard against the onslaught of personal immaturity overtaking us, it's essential that you recognize these trends. They define how we personally cooperate with the hideous strength to create adult brats.

PROLONGED ADOLESCENCE:
WHEN IS GROWN UP "GROWN UP"?

One of the effects of the hideous strength is that it has influenced us to rub out the line between adolescence and adulthood.

It is regrettable that the social structure in the United States has lost the large-scale impact of the military-induced personal maturation process, for nothing has replaced it as a wholesale benchmark for measuring progress from adolescence into adulthood. Without a yardstick, it has become easy for the adolescent maturation process to slip into adult-age years, a postponement that more often leaves employers asking the same question as many parents. *Is my child [my employee or employee applicant] really grown up?*

The Latin root word for adolescence is *adolescere*, meaning "to grow into maturity." But if we have little against which to determine that growth, then all that's left is our own opinion of maturity. That's called relativism, and that's bad for business because businesses rely on knowing the quantitative measure of human capital; they cannot depend on guesswork.

The new trend makes it increasingly difficult to identify an acceptable time line to adulthood. As noted, there was a time when employers assumed that young job applicants automatically possessed a healthy degree of emotional maturity. Not now, particularly in light of the obfuscation between adult desires and adolescent delusion brought to us by the newest crop of workforce entrants—young people roughly between the ages of seventeen and twenty-seven.

Take Jocelyn S. Kirsch. Better known as the female half of the "Bonnie and Clyde" jet-setters, Kirsch was convicted at age twenty-two of stealing the identities of sixteen people to finance an expensive globe-hopping lifestyle with her twenty-five-year-old boyfriend, Edward Anderton. A smart, beautiful, well-liked student at Drexel University, Kirsch threw away a promising future for a year of opulent, self-indulgent living at the expense of others.

Kirsch's attorney, Ronald Greenblat, said this about Kirsch's mistake: "She's supposed to be graduating college right now, and instead she's going to be going down to federal court in a few weeks and entering a plea."[3] Yes, she should have been graduating from college—at least under the old rules of society when graduation carried with it the presumption of personal maturity. Instead, Kirsch serves as an example of what can happen when early adult-age adolescence is perceived by her generation as permissible.

The alternative for Kirsch and her boyfriend? That was voiced by US Attorney Patrick Meehan, who said, "If they had worked half as hard at their careers as they did in these multiple schemes, they would have been remarkably successful."[4] But that would have involved acting like a responsible adult—so uncool at their age.

Columnist Kay S. Hymowitz captured the essence of the fuzzy transitional battle between adolescence and adulthood, describing how twenty-something women struggle to find mature men their age. She calls the male version of this struggle the "child-man," describing men who exist "in a new hybrid state of semi-hormonal adolescence and responsible self-reliance."

Painting a painfully accurate picture of the child-man, she writes, "Now meet the twenty-first-century you, also twenty-six. You've finished college and work in a cubicle in a large Chicago financial-services firm. You live in an apartment with a few single guy friends. In your spare time, you play basketball with your buddies, download the latest indie songs from iTunes, have some fun with the Xbox 360, take a leisurely shower, massage some product into your hair and face—and then it's off to bars and parties, where you meet, and often bed, girls of widely varied hues and sizes."[5] Ouch!

Emily Meehan of the *Wall Street Journal* online writes about young professionals and their strong desire to travel while unencumbered by life's obligations—family, job, community involvement. You know, adult things. We're not talking one- or two-week vacations, mind you, but the extended type of leisurely travel that typically prohibits one from holding a job.

She tells the story of Miro Kazakoff, twenty-five, a management consulting professional who grew ambivalent about what to do in his life. He could have stayed in his job, but when a friend offered him an opportunity to take time off and travel for nine months, he jumped at the opportunity. Said Kazakoff, "I wasn't enthused about anything in life."[6] He could have said, "Nothing is forcing me to be a responsibly employed adult at this time, so what the heck. Let's travel and party."

Now, here's the kicker. When Kazakoff returned to the job market, do you think he listed his trip on his résumé? Nope. He hid it—a practice endorsed by a career counselor Meehan cites in the same article. After all, he wouldn't want a prospective employer to know that he quit a good job after three years to participate in a rolling party because he was unenthused about life.

Somewhere in the catacombs of my Boomer mind, there's a mental image of Ferris Bueller taking more than a day off, attempting to trick authority into believing he's a good kid, fully knowing that self-discipline and responsible behavior aren't required of him. Why grow up? Adolescence is good. I think I'll take it with me.

MUDDLED ADOLESCENCE: WHAT IS NORMAL?

Another influence of the hideous strength of our social system factors is the blurring of what we now define as a normal adolescence.

It is easier to understand why the transition period between adolescence and adulthood has become severely skewed when you realize how low we've set the behavioral bar—what we consider normal behavior—for adolescence. Never before have adolescents faced so much ground to make up in the maturation process. This handicap is another factor contributing to the creation of adult brats, since lower behavioral standards for adolescents translate into lower expectations for adult behavior.

This deviance from normalcy is enabled by social perceptions, the most powerful of which are promulgated by parents and the media. Parenting standards for teens have fallen into lockstep with the media's warped portrayal of normal adolescence. Take the story of Meaghan Bosch, a twenty-one-year-old Southern Methodist University student who tragically died of a drug overdose after falling in with the wrong crowd. This is how columnist Trey Garrison of *D Magazine* describes Meaghan's upbringing in an upper-class suburb near Dallas:

> Like any normal kid, she got in trouble, too. She went to beer parties and occasionally smoked pot. She and a close friend would sometimes sneak a few pours out of her parents' liquor cabinet, then run through the sprinklers on the golf course behind the house. They rolled people's houses. When she and a friend were 14, they vowed not to enter high school without having kissed a boy. So they went to the movie theater and did just that to a couple of boys they met. Later, in high school, her cell phone never seemed to stop ringing. Boys she dated fell in love with her in the span of days, not weeks or months.[7]

Did I miss something here, or did Garrison paint a picture of normal adolescence as drinking, drugging, criminal mischief, and sexual promiscuity? See the lowered standard?

Here's a quick quiz. Name the last non-G-rated movie you saw in which adolescents are portrayed as something other than messed-up, confused victims of social forces beyond their control. Hard, isn't it? Can't you sense how young impressionable minds, barraged by this warped depiction of their stage of life, come to believe the image?

But what happens when parents buy into the media's image? Then you get Joy Miller, whose willingness to lower the behavioral standards for her nineteen-year-old bank-robbing daughter, Ashley Miller, led her to deny that her daughter did anything wrong, even though the robbery was videotaped. You may remember the criminals, whom the media dubbed the "Barbie Bandits." Ashley and her friend, Heather Johnston, both nineteen, walked into an Atlanta-area bank, giggled like airheads, and robbed the bank in conjunction with a male bank teller friend.

Appearing on ABC's *Good Morning America* shortly after the robbery, Miller said of her daughter, "I want [people] to know that her and Heather are not bandits. They're little girls that made a bad choice." With parents like this, no wonder young people enter the workforce thinking that their aberrant behaviors are normal and that they aren't bad employees when they misbehave.

I've worked with many troubled youths and met my fair share of parents in denial, so it's not hard for me to believe that Miller fails to recognize the boundary for acceptable adolescent behavior. The greater danger is the failure of the ABC interviewer to ask any follow-up question to point out Miller's delusion.

You or I might have asked in retort, "But Ms. Miller, your daughter is in jail, and there is videotaped evidence showing the crime. If this is not the action of a criminal, what is? Isn't nineteen an age at which kids should be held accountable as adults?" Ah, but that would go against the media's unconscious attempt to dumb down adolescence. It's better if we can keep the expectation levels low and get a shot of a parent crying over an age of innocence that doesn't exist.

I'm compelled to step aside for a moment and speak to parents who, like Joy Miller, may unadvisedly live in this fantasy land of media-made adolescence. This may be a business book, but business success and the social forces of our society are inextricably intertwined. So here goes.

If you are a parent of a kid in trouble or one who constantly pushes parental boundaries and, like Miller, you think of your kid as a good kid, I challenge you to rethink your opinion. I know it's hard to do because you're emotionally wrapped up in the situation. But I want you to quit basing your present opinion of your child's behavior on some sentimental image of a far-removed time when your sweet child was in kindergarten, before being victimized by an amoral society. Turn off the syrupy propaganda of the media (except for Dr. Phil) and listen to two words of advice: wake up! And two more: get real! Your child may be a bad kid, doing bad things, but society has hoodwinked you into believing that bad is normal. I promise you, if you snap back to reality, then somewhere, sometime in your child's future, a business manager will thank you.

BAD PARENTING: THE ENABLERS

In overreacting to the hideous strength of systemic changes in our society, parents have adopted two extreme approaches to parenting, both of which produce immature adults. I call these forms of poor parenting *hyperparenting* and *hypoparenting*. One approach looks at parenting from a hands-on, manic, I-can-help-my-child-beat-the-system viewpoint; the other believes that the system places too many odds against them, resulting in an I-can't-do-anything-to-help-my-kid defeatist mentality. Surprisingly, while one strategy may seem a surefire means to helping a child avoid adult immaturity and the other doesn't, both produce their fair share of workplace brats.

The Hyperparent

Hyperparenting involves parents going to any extreme to secure life, liberty, and guaranteed happiness for their child, not just the opportunity to pursue such. Hyperparents mistake the pursuit of excellence for the pursuit of happiness. Of course excellence can result in happiness, but when children are pushed, pulled, and preached into the belief that happiness will come only through achieving their parents' expectations of excellence in the highest order, then a relational disconnect with the parent often follows. The door is opened wide for the creation of a social misfit.

Like many members of the "greatest generation," my father feared that the social movement of the 1960s would turn me into an irresponsible hippy. To ensure that I pursued his concept of excellence, he rigidly planned my life goals and lifestyle. Hairstyle, clothes, friends, schools, church—everything was orchestrated by him, no exception. As an obedient son, I complied.

Dad wanted me to be an engineer, so off to college I went to study engineering. Several things stood in my way, particularly my inability to pass math class. After a year of futile pursuit of my dad's educational mandate, I returned home to tell him I wanted to study forestry. After a lengthy, often contentious debate, my father surprisingly gave in to my choice. But in doing so, he threw the college catalog at me and said sarcastically, "Go ahead. Major in forestry. But I don't know how your wife and children will ever be proud of you."

His words still hurt today. The emotional hole in our relationship that he created lasted until the day he died. And even though I became a scholarship forestry student and used my degree to help many needy kids in my wilderness camp program, I never felt the accomplishment was good enough to satisfy my dad. In his mind, I was always a misfit.

Columnist David Brooks aptly describes the damaging effect of hypercontrol parenting, be it "helicopter parents," "tethered parents," or whatever is the *nom du jour*. Calling the effect a "rank-link imbalance," he states that an inherent developmental danger is incurred by those who pursue their parents' demands of excellence without learning how to build normal, non-performance-based relationships. According to Brooks, these beleaguered children will end up as adults who possess "all of the social skills required to improve their social rank, but none of the social skills that lead to genuine bonding." Such type-A achievers, driven to success by parents who overreact to the social system of their time, end up awash in self-destructing "accumulated narcissism" that is "too much to bear" for others around them. Isolated, they become what Brooks calls "kings of the emotionally avoidant. Because of disuse, their sensitivity synapses are still performing at preschool levels."[8]

If you've paid attention at all to my description of delinquency, you should recognize the syndrome described by Brooks. Hyperparents put their innocent children on a path to becoming delinquent adults.

The Hypoparent

At the other end of the spectrum are hypoparents practicing a form of partial or deficient child rearing. This approach to parenting ranges from those who incorrectly think that having a child living under their roof automatically constitutes good parenting to those who completely abandon their child to the care of others. One extreme, second-chance parenting, involves parents in thinking that as long as an adult child lives with them, there is always an opportunity to correct their parenting mistakes. The other adopts a helpless "poor me" philosophy of parenting in which the best parents can do to help their child fight the system is to relinquish their parenting role to wiser people.

Second-chance or "open nest" parenting is a growing trend. Since 1980, the proportion of eighteen- to thirty-four-year-olds living in open-nest homes has grown by 5 percent, to roughly 34 percent.[9] This represents a disturbing trend that undermines the need of young adults to complete the maturation process and function as healthy independent beings.

Hypoparents who embrace the opportunity of second-chance parenting do their children more harm than good. One parent of a twenty-six-year-old son who came home from college without a career plan coaxed his son into pursuit of a different career path requiring additional education. During this schooling, the parent allowed his son to live at home but also admitted his son's need to be more focused. The father justified his enablement of his son's prolonged entry into adulthood based on the need of his child to feel happy. He also said, "He's a good friend. We enjoy having him [home]."[10]

I thought it was a parent's duty to rear an adult, not a friend. Can you imagine this child applying for a job, seeking a supervisor who will be his friend, not his boss, and make him feel at home?

Listen to the enlightened confession of Kelli Renfrow, who at age twenty-eight swallowed hard and cut the cord by moving out of her enabling parents' home. "I was always willing to assert my adulthood, *as long as it didn't cost me anything.* And I'm not just talking money. I wanted my mistakes to have a net under them. I wanted someone to take care of me. And I definitely wanted approval. Little did I know, going without those things is what makes you independent." Welcome to adulthood, Kelli! She now admits that life's struggles "are much more promising when you're facing forward instead of homeward."[11]

Then there are the hypoparents who feel that the hideous strength of our social system outweighs their ability to function as responsible adults, so they surrender their duty to others. In its most extreme forms, this consists of the forced removal of a child from the parental home because of abuse or neglect. Employers looking for relief from the onslaught of worker immaturity should be alarmed by the sheer number of children abandoned to be reared by other, less invested adults. Census data indicate that more than 2.5 million children—future employees with increased potential of problematic behavior—are being raised by grandparents or other relatives. Called the "skip generation," these kids are literally being forced into the caring lap of Boomers, many of whom resent being called into parenting for the second time.[12]

Too many are like Jessielean Smith, whose daughter was headed to a four-year prison sentence, leaving her mother with the unruly grandchildren left behind. Confronting her crying daughter in jail, the elder Smith barked at her daughter, "Don't cry—I'm the one crying! Your little boy's jumping all up over my foot. My hand ain't no good. My blood pressure's high. And I'm obese. I don't want to hear you're depressed. I'm depressed!"[13]

Poor kids. Barring a miracle, some employer will one day likely have to pay the price for their abandonment and their grandmother's misery.

Even among the nearly half million children who annually reside in foster care, the implications for business are not good. In 2013, the average length of time a child spent in foster care was fourteen months—two months longer than a decade earlier.[14] During this time, many foster children become emotionally desensitized by repeated drifting from family to family, without a permanent home. Coping consists of developing a self-centered sense of survival. Bringing the traumatic remnants of this emotionally withdrawn, self-centered, and nomadic lifestyle with them to the workplace can present severe challenges to coworkers and managers, particularly in light of the diminished capability of business to offer the stability of employment such workers may seek.

Three million or more kids, future employees, are being reared by nonbiological "parents" substituting for irresponsible hypoparents. Three million. That's greater than the single population of twenty-six US states and territories.

As these victims of poor parenting enter the labor force, the price for parental overreaction to the hideous strength will be paid.

Narcissism: It's My Party and I'll Cry If I Want To

The cumulative effect of the various elements of the hideous strength drives us to shun the pursuit of deep interpersonal relationships in favor of narcissistic ones.

It shouldn't surprise you that the hideous strength contributes significantly to the onslaught of toxic self-centered employees in today's workplace. Every element of its power encourages us to exchange personal sacrifice for ignoble self-interest:

- A military that, until recently, pandered to the concept of "an Army of one."
- A government system that encourages us to selfishly grovel to secure remedies for one person's needs over another's.
- Schools that tell children they're great even when they are not.
- Communication technology that allows us to put ourselves front and center on the world stage in an instant.
- Businesses that must compete with each other, often in a cutthroat manner, to retain the loyalty of each employee.
- Fractured families that force their children to become individuals lost in the middle of parental division.

You should be concerned how deeply ingrained this narcissistic trend has become in the social fabric of the labor force. In the past, we have tolerated the occasional self-absorbed line-level employee who cost us a few extra cents per product unit. But now the egocentricity of the American worker has reached the bastion of business professionals, in some cases robbing us of personal health and well-being in the process.

Such revelation came as a shock to doctors in the Rochester, New York, area whose nonbeneficial self-disclosure (read: talking about themselves to patients) was identified as a health concern in a study on patient care and outcomes published in the *Archives of Internal Medicine*. Analyzing secret audio recordings of bogus patients who visited one hundred primary care physicians in the Rochester area over a one-year period, the study's authors "discovered that doctors talked about themselves in a third of the audio recordings and that there was no evidence that any of the doctors' disclosures about themselves helped patients or established rapport."[15]

So what? I can't imagine my dad—an oral surgeon—being a great communicator either, particularly when I was a kid and he worked on my teeth. I didn't fall for his line "Son, this is going to hurt me more than it hurts you" when he stuck a long needle in my mouth.

What is damaging to patient care in the Rochester study is the conclusion of the lead author of the study. "We were quite shocked," she said. "We realized that maybe not 100 percent of the time, but most of the time self-disclosure had more to do with [the physicians] than with the patients."

Eighty percent of the time that a physician initiated self-disclosure with a patient, the doctor lost track of the subject under discussion before the interruption. Another of the study's authors stated, "Then the patient ends up having to take care of the doctor and then the question is who should be paying whom. We looked for any statement of comfort, any statement of appreciation, any deepening of the conversation." None was found.[16]

This kind of one-sided invitation to "enter my world without me having to enter yours" is outrageously evident in the plethora of Internet social networking sites that scream, "Look at me, but don't touch me" or "Listen to my opinion while I ignore yours." These invitations to pseudo-relationships involve little more than an individual retreating into a safe emotional shell, then opening himself up like a peep show for limited, noncommittal examination. We've regressed from building beneficial two-way interpersonal relationships to preferring *enterpersonal* ones where relationships are one-way.

The force that influences us to such narcissism is powerful and ultimately self-defeating. Just ask Santa Barbara, California, defense lawyer Steve Balash. Before one of his clients was sentenced, Balash asked her to remove damaging pictures of herself from her Internet social media page. His client had been convicted of vehicular manslaughter while driving drunk. One of her photos showed the twenty-two-year-old fool holding a beer bottle. Others depicted her drinking with friends at a local lounge—all in the months following her crime.[17]

The client refused Balash's request, giving prosecutors enough ammunition to secure a longer prison term. I hope you agree that the attention-seeking freedom to exercise such enter-personal folly isn't worth the confinement without freedom that Balash's adult brat received from the court. And I also hope you recognize that the same social force is creating a new set of employee management difficulties where the boundary between healthy employee self-expression and egomaniacal manipulation of coworkers is razor thin. Problem employees love to take advantage of such confusion.

Take crying in the workplace. I know I'm on thin ice here with the more emotional types, but employee crying is a hot button management issue, particularly with a younger generation that feels entitled to express itself.

Put yourself in the shoes of Kathy Lyle, fifty-five, an accounting firm owner whose thirty-something employee broke out in tears when she was told to install a software program on her computer. When Lyle asked the employee why she was crying, the employee replied, "You scare me." Lyle's response was to tell the employee to pull herself together.[18]

How about Kathryn Brady, thirty-four, a corporate finance manager who tends to cry when she becomes frustrated working with difficult people. She defends her weepy nature, saying, "The misinterpretation that I'm whiny or weak is just not fair."[19]

Then there's the twenty-something male coworker of Bonnie Sashin, fifty-six, who fought back tears when he received a tongue-lashing from a colleague. Sashin admires her colleague's ability to be genuine, saying, "A guy less in touch with his feelings . . . might have expressed anger, outrage or pounded the table,"[20] as if anger is a disingenuous emotion to be avoided whereas weeping is acceptable.

The question to be asked is, what is the worker attempting to achieve with tears or any other emotional display? Delinquents on my wilderness camping trips cried often, provoked by both the harsh outdoor environment and the antics of similarly minded campmates. The trick was to discern whether the emotional outburst was genuine or whether it was purposefully designed to manipulate others.

The strong social forces that now push our society toward rampant relational egotism cause me to believe the latter about many of today's workers. Ms. Sashin, you've been had.

Impersonal Empowerment: It's Nothing Personal

Because the hideous strength has convinced us that "it's all about me," there is no "you" to consider.

Raise your hand if you've heard this phrase (or something like it) within the last few days: "It's nothing personal." Okay, you can put it down.

How did I know? you ask.

Simple. The phrase has become wildly popular, used extensively to excuse the far-flung exercise of narcissism described earlier.

Undercut a colleague on your job to make yourself look better? That's okay. It isn't personal; it's business.

Pilfer a few bucks from the office petty cash fund that pays for morning donuts? It won't hurt anybody.

Inflate the number of service hours charged a customer? Hey, they can afford it. Nothing personal against them.

Perhaps you remember Slade Woodson, the confused nineteen-year-old Virginia man who was arrested in spring 2008 for firing on five vehicles on Interstate 64, wounding two people. Woodson is a social misfit whose erratic behavior leading up to his heinous crime is widely known to those in his rural hometown.

In 2007, Woodson was charged with auto theft and arson when he burned two vehicles he had stolen, one of which belonged to family friend Norman Carter. Woodson later attempted to apologize to Carter, writing a note, "It was nothing personal, it was just something that happened."[21] With the apology, Carter naively thought the young man's problems were behind him.

Mark it down, folks. If you ever hear people try to excuse their poor behavior under the guise of "It's nothing personal," they're exhibiting the emotional withdrawal pattern of delinquents; and they've been influenced to act that way by the systemic social forces of our time.

On my camping trips with delinquent youth, the first battle the counselors always fought with the campers was over their tendency to depersonalize others. Initial group problem-solving sessions, called *huddle-ups*, typically included many exhortations for kids to stop calling each other "dude" or other aloof monikers. Little could be accomplished to correct an individual's personal behavior until a perspective of recognizing each other as feeling human beings was established.

It's frightening when I hear the same impersonal babble repeated by modern-day industry managers. At a maritime conference, I heard a veteran boat captain offer his solution to the excessive personnel turnover problem hounding his industry's younger deck crew employees. Noting the tendency of deck crew members to become attached to girlfriends who influence the deck crew employees to quit their jobs, the officer suggested "getting rid of girlfriends." Honest. His proposal was greeted with a round of prolonged applause.

Before you blow off this story as typical of crusty maritime officers, I've heard the same sentiment expressed by the manager of an ultramodern manufacturing plant and a technician manager at a high-tech defense missile assembly plant. The depth to which we feel impersonal empowerment now appears to know no bounds.

As with enterpersonal relationships, the advent of wireless and Internet communication technology has increased the availability of faceless, impersonal communication techniques. If you don't like your neighbors and want to say something bad about them without them knowing who said it, a popular web site allows you to anonymously voice your opinion to all the world, regardless of its truth.

How about telling that person you've dated a few times that you don't want to see her again, but you don't want the aggravation or embarrassment of telling her personally. Simple: there's a phone service that allows your phone call to skip directly to her voice mailbox where you can leave a message without risk of talking to the person you called. After all, there's no need to consider the other person, is there? The service also benefits employees who want to call their manager to excuse their absence from work but don't want to talk to the manager personally. It's none of their business anyway, right?

Perhaps the one-sided pursuit of impersonality reached its zenith with the introduction by Sega Toys of a femalelike robot called EMA, Eternal Maiden Actualization. Designed as big busted, petite, friendly, and—most importantly—battery powered, she/it is described as "very lovable, and though she's not a human, she can act like a real girlfriend."[22] Now if they can teach it not to call everyone "dude," maybe they're onto something.

WONDERFULLY BLEAK

Okay, I hear you screaming. I'll stop listing the onslaught of seemingly unconquerable systemic and personal factors that stand in the way of ridding your workplace of jerks. No doubt you think the picture is bleak, the chances slim of defeating the hideous strength that drives adult brat behavior at work. The odds appear stacked against you.

What work culture can resist the influence that causes people to prolong their adolescence in pursuit of folly, to dumb down the definition of adolescence to the lowest norm, to parent their children in a way that renders them social misfits, to prefer unhealthy one-sided relationships instead of mutually beneficial ones, and to develop an intense self-obsession that becomes an excuse for treating others impersonally?

Art Rollins felt helpless to fight such things when he called me in 1992 to help him with his rebellious workers. Every parent or caseworker who contacted my wilderness program felt the same about his or her ward. Frankly, so have I at times, such as during my predicament with John Morton. It's that sickening feeling that accompanies the realization that I cannot influence or control others when they desperately need it.

Control. Up until this point, I've used the word sparingly. Some see it as a threatening word, emitting undertones of the power to restrain someone or something—so un-American.

But control is essential, serving as the foundational cause of all loss, according to Frank Bird's loss causation model. Lack of control, or a deficient system of control measures, is what allows the hideous strength of our social system factors to develop and our personal factors to be unduly influenced in a negative way. *Adult brats are created and exist in the workplace because there is no control to stop the factors that cause them.*

The hideous strength and its influence on us are like a seemingly impenetrable mountain range. Your task as a businessperson is to climb into and over that range to discover the solutions that can free your workplace of jerks. Doing so will require that you exercise all the self-control you can muster, and it will challenge your ability to control others on your expedition.

The rewards of taking control will become apparent as you push yourself and your team into the rarified air where few dare to go. Along the way, you will find the three essential business values—honesty, loyalty, compassion—that we have allowed adult brats to kidnap and hide in seemingly unreachable crags and cliffs. Rescuing these lost values and putting them to use for you and your business will empower you to overcome the hideous strength and quell the crisis of personal immaturity in your workplace.

Before you begin your rescue effort, consider the following three questions. Think of them as your premountaineering safety checklist.

1. Are You Scared?

If the thought of challenging adult brats in your workplace doesn't frighten you, it should. There hasn't been one instance of helping a client fight this battle when, at some point, I haven't felt out of my league, intimidated to the core. The strength of the root causes of loss we are fighting against is great.

You will do best if you recall the famous words of Jedi Master Yoda to his trainee Luke Skywalker. Luke tells Yoda, "I won't fail you. I'm not afraid." Then Yoda replies, "You will be. You will be." Expect at one point or another to feel as if you are losing the battle.

2. Do You Know Where You Are Going?

In chapters 4 and 5, we've explored the root causes of adult brat behavior. These causes collectively act as a map to help you negotiate the mountain range of undesired behavior in your workplace. If you don't use the map, or can't interpret its symbols correctly, you can easily become lost in your journey to restore responsible behavior to your business. Remember Tom, the counselor who led my camp group on a misleading, painful sidetrack? Don't do the same.

If you aren't sure you can recognize what causes bad behavior, review each factor and take notes. Ask yourself, where have I seen this factor resulting in poor employee behavior? Doing this will greatly diminish the danger of your being detoured onto unproductive paths.

3. Do You Know Your Team?

Undertaking a perilous trip through the mountains with dubious sidekicks can be fatal. You need to distinguish friend from foe, who is on your side in the fight against the jerks and who isn't. If you are unclear about what a responsible adult employee looks like, then you need to go back and review chapter 3, "A Dark Heart." Take notes, and be aware what type of person you climb with.

It's Time To Climb

The overarching motto of wilderness camping is "Prepare by instruction; learn by experience." In the area of preparation, you now have a huge advantage to take with you on your climb into correcting your business's worker maturity issues. You know where we are out of control and what forces are causing this effect.

As for learning by experience, it's time for you to quit contemplating the climb and do it, rescuing values in the process.

Part Two

The Fix

Beating the Brats

Chapter Six
Using Guile and Guts

Anne Whiteman knows what it feels like to summit the mountain range you have to climb. As one of the most famous whistleblowers of our young century, Whiteman dared to call attention to management-driven safety lapses in air traffic controller practices at Dallas-Fort Worth International Airport (DFW).

For Whiteman, it was the equivalent of climbing Mount Everest, where lungs sear from thin air, muscles ache from oxygen deprivation, and the mind struggles to overcome the necessary mental cruelty that drives one to reach the summit. Sacrifice is expected.

As a Federal Aviation Administration (FAA) controller working DFW's control facility, Whiteman repeatedly called to her supervisors' attention what she felt was a pattern of operational lapses that endangered fliers. In her opinion, air control managers were covering up incidents in which aircraft were flying too closely to one another, manipulating the reporting system so that pilots were blamed instead of controllers.

Frustrated by her unresponsive supervisors and concerned for public safety, Whiteman turned whistle-blower. Her thanks from colleagues consisted of a series of retaliatory measures straight from the KGB handbook. Says Whiteman, "A guy (coworker) used to knock me down at work all the time. He'd walk by—if nobody was looking, he'd knock me down."[1]

Attempts at payback also included running Whiteman off the road, declaring her medically unfit for duty, locking her in an office, and pasting dimes to her belongings. In no uncertain terms, she was made to feel an outcast among coworkers.

The personal toll for standing up to the jerks in her workplace was heavy. For her husband, Gary, also an air traffic controller, it meant exercising a level of personal restraint that I'm not sure I could muster. Whiteman admits she used to draw strength from telling herself she "would do it again." Now, she says, "I'm not so sure." In a rare moment of self-pity, she says, "I'll never be the same 'ole Annie again."[2]

Bolstered by the testimony of a coworker, Whiteman's complaints were eventually recognized as valid by the FAA. Two managers in her operations were reassigned and the FAA promised change in its work culture. Still, nothing can remove the emotional scars or the physical weariness of the lengthy battle fought by Anne Whiteman. Mountain climbing is difficult at best.

Before we go any further, let's get something straight. I'm not asking you or telling you to be a whistle-blower, nor to act like one. But in recovering the values stolen from your business or work environment by adult brats, you may feel like a whistle-blower.

Whistle-blowing is necessary when a work environment becomes so blind to its own corrupting culture that nothing apart from a closeted appeal to a higher authority can remedy it. Perhaps that is your case, or at least you may feel as if it is. Like Anne Whiteman, you work in an authoritarian work culture of rigid rules and indisputable management hierarchy. Your only option to express serious concern is to step outside that framework and use whatever legal protection you have available.

But if you are an employee of a mid- to small-size business, or if you are a small business owner, speaking up is a less cumbersome process than it was for Anne Whiteman. Returning the lost values of honesty, loyalty, and compassion to your workplace—putting them to work in your battle against adult brats—is easier in that respect. There are three rules you can follow to *guarantee* victory in your battle.

Straight Shooting

Sound confident, don't I? That's because the three rules are crafted from twenty years' experience in turning around the lives of troubled youth. During that experience, the delinquents taught me what to do to help them and what boundaries they needed to curb their destructive behaviors. Accomplished physicians listen long and hard to patients with a resistant disease because the patient's input often leads to the remedy. Today's problematic employees so closely resemble the troubled kids of yesterday that the restrictions those kids needed then should be the rules that business needs to implement now.

As discussed in detail in chapters 6, 7, and 8, these three rules provide a system of behavioral influence that is an antidote to the influence of the hideous strength. Followed properly, they stop us from collectively straying to the personal path of immaturity that negative social forces encourage. By applying these rules in both your work environment and your personal life, you won't need a bevy of impractical, complicated employee management policies designed to help you dance around the issue of right and wrong employee behavior. You can meet problem employees head-on and win.

Before you think this is too good to be true, I confess that I and my fellow wilderness program staff members made many mistakes leading up to the formulation of these rules. Back in 1977, there were no training classes on how to help troubled kids in the wilderness. I know; I searched in vain for such assistance. Don't think for a moment that I don't regret attempting to use "confrontation therapy" with a gang member while rock climbing in an Oklahoma wilderness area. I couldn't run fast enough from him. Then there's the time I acted like a drill sergeant, forcing a kid to do push-ups as punishment for throwing rocks. Now that was a really innovative use of the wilderness environment. What a dope I was.

Gradually, though, we achieved success through the framework of three minimalist "rules of the trail." Success using them in the wilderness translated into success when I adapted them for use in the workplace.

When Art Rollins called me to help him correct his out-of-control employees, the three rules of the trail became the guiding principles I used to help his trucking company. Within two years of implementing the principles embodied in these rules, Art documented substantial improvement in both employee compliance and loyalty. He trimmed his 41 percent personnel turnover rate down to 2 percent during that period and reaped a savings of at least $250,000 in related personnel turnover costs for his 120 employees. Gains in behavioral compliance were reflected in a 46 percent reduction in his total injury index rate.

Are these rules lightning in a bottle, the answer to gross systemic employee character issues? Follow them, and you be the judge. See if they help you climb the mountain range of employee problems that confront you. All I can do is point the way, showing you how they help bring about maturity in troubled kids and like-minded employees. I first give you the rule as I used it with my campers; then I illustrate how it can help build successful adult brat-free businesses.

Keep this in mind: as a stipulation for enrollment in my program, each camper signed an agreement to abide by all three rules. As you may have gathered, my charges didn't always honor their commitments. Even so, a high expectation for obedience to the rules was established from the beginning. The agreement to follow these rules was the only pretrip document that a camper was required to sign.

RULE 1: SIGHT AND SOUND

The rule of transparency: *You must stay within sight and sound of the camp group at all times unless given permission by a counselor.*

Sounds like Big Brother is watching, doesn't it? Indeed, this rule helped camp counselors keep track of camper movement, if only for safety purposes. But if supervision is the primary function you ascribe to this rule, then you've made the common mistake of confusing the principle of transparency with the act of observation. You've also discerned the wrong motive for weaving transparency into the effort to stop bad behavior.

Transparency is necessary to expose troubled individuals to what will help them, to influence them for the better, not just to catch them doing what is wrong. It is not simply an audit, a surprise inspection, a 24/7 surveillance program, or any other such measure designed for higher authorities to see what's going on with their charges. It is more.

Transparency is a principle of healthy two-way human interaction in which we are free, without fear of exploitation, to reveal what we think or feel with those we choose. In a genuinely transparent organization, transparency surpasses rank or authority, allowing candid self-disclosure to travel equally up and down the chain of command. I call this uphill and downhill transparency. Uphill transparency takes place when those of lower rank or status can easily discern the true feelings, behavior, motives, and values of those who rank above them. Downhill transparency is the reverse.

In my wilderness program, the sight-and-sound rule provided uphill transparency by allowing self-defeating, emotionally insincere kids to easily access a constant model of responsible values— the behavior of camp counselors. This exposure was not without cost. Counselors not only were required to obey the three rules, but were also tasked with modeling the rules beyond reproach. Bearing this strain for twenty-one to twenty-eight straight days, in front of annoying kids, created enough emotional trauma to warrant a camping trip of its own.

After each trip, when the campers returned home, I witnessed many ways in which counselors released the 24/7 pressure of uphill transparency, born of the call to model behavioral excellence. Some withdrew into a fortress of solitude, hanging a Do Not Disturb sign on their emotional door. Others eschewed behavioral caution, displaying a temporary wild streak until responsibility returned.

In one memorable case, a female counselor and her coworkers celebrated with a meal at an upscale Denver restaurant designed to mimic the cliffs of Acapulco. A cliff-diving exhibition was the night's scheduled entertainment, but it turned out to be provided by the counselor instead of the professional divers employed by the restaurant.

I can empathize with the counselor. The first time our camp program used the sight-and-sound rule was when I served as the lead counselor for a trip involving a group of so-called first-time offenders from the Dallas County (Texas) Juvenile Department. (Really, they were first-time gettin' caughters, multiple-time offenders.)

Within the first twenty-four hours of the trip, the rule of transparency paid dividends, just as it will quickly work in your workplace. When it did, both the pressure and the power I felt from uphill transparency was positively staggering, just as it will be for you when you try it.

To prepare you adequately for the experience, I need to take you back to the moment early in the trip when Beto Martinez opened the door for you to successfully rid your workplace of people like him.

BETO

There was little about Beto Martinez that looked different from your garden-variety teen. Small for age fifteen, with curly, sand-colored hair and a freckled face, the youth possessed a magnetic personality that caused others to seek his companionship. Most dangerous of all was his disarming Tom Sawyer-like smile, causing others to place their confidence in his bruised, confused heart.

Smiles can hide a great deal. Just looking at him, it was difficult to discern the deep scars he had developed as he grew up in Texas under the hindrance of his heritage. Beto's life had been a cruelty magnified by the combination of the pointedly Hispanic name of his father and the physical looks derived from his Anglo mother. Considering the cultural deck stacked against him, his parents' divorce, and the frequency with which immature adolescents trade verbal jabs about children of mixed-race marriages, Beto might as well have worn a sign that said, "Hit me."

Beto was fully enveloped in this confusion by the time his group of offenders enrolled for the wilderness trip. His attempts to emotionally distance himself from his mother deeply hurt her. During our pretrip interview, the fear that she somehow had not been an effective or loving parent was racking her with guilt. "I would like my son to become a little more responsible and caring for others," she said in a quiet, desperate plea. "If he would only apply himself to do what he is capable of doing." Her near-prayerful petition gave me the impression that, if only Beto could be convinced to make up his bed each day as he had done as a small child, she would consider it a major victory.

Knowing this, it was easy to understand why there was something wrong with the eagerness with which Beto offered his smile. Smiling, along with an occasional petty theft to prove his self-worth, had become Beto's defense mechanism against all the troubles he felt life had dealt him. For the most part, his smiles had served him well. At one point, however, he had chosen to steal from the wrong source—the son of an influential local politician. This feat overwhelmed his charming defense. He was placed on probation, then enrolled for my trip. As an added bonus, I enlisted a special trip counselor: Carol Smith, Beto's probation officer.

AWAKENING THE BEAR OF TRANSPARENCY

Beto's trip began with rain, the kind of bone-chilling mountain downpour that can quickly induce hypothermia. Judging by the molasses-like pace of Beto's campmates as they awakened in the damp Mora River Valley and stood in the rain without donning their rain gear, they didn't much care. Considering we were only a half day into our journey, the group was well into the "learning by experience" stage, having ignored all my "preparation by instruction." Still, the day was young—breakfast had not been eaten—and there was hope that the day would yet bring sunshine. Ha!

Suddenly the shrill voice of Bridgette Kleghorn, one of Beto's fellow first-time gettin' caughters, pierced the quiet of the 8,500-foot-high mountain valley. "He stole it! He stole it!" she screamed, setting off echoes miles away. At the end of her pointed finger stood Beto, flashing his incredulous smile of innocence. Not a bad acting job, and it would have worked if it weren't for the crumbs and jelly he had on his face. From the looks of it, Beto had stolen the group's breakfast from Bridgette's backpack, and there would be hell to pay from his camp group.

There the story would end if only the downhill aspect of transparency were considered. Because of the sight-and-sound rule, Beto's misdeed had been committed and revealed in full sight of the group. "Busted" was the way John Morton had put it when caught violating the rules on one of my trips ten years earlier.

But in the interim, we had made a quantum leap in fully capitalizing on the principle of transparency. On the one hand, Morton was introduced to the use of downhill transparency as a punitive tool. For being busted, he received some form of ineffective physical punishment. Push-ups were assigned, if I remember correctly. The only principle he learned from the experience was *Don't get caught the next time.*

Beto, on the other hand, was afforded the opportunity to experience both downhill and uphill transparency. In addition to being busted (downhill), he was required to immediately participate in a group problem-solving session (uphill) in which the group determined his discipline and, hopefully, gave guidance to set him on a path to better behavior. As you may imagine, in the initial stages of the trip the group was heavily dependent on the input of responsible counselors to monitor healthy boundaries for discipline and to suggest helpful counsel for the group to give the offender.

Therein lay the problem. I was cold, hungry, and getting wet (despite my comfy Gore-Tex rain suit)—just like everyone in our group—because this bonehead had decided to steal and eat *my* breakfast food in front of God and country. Jeez, I wanted to give the guy a ton of push-ups as punishment for eating my food, then push his rear end on up the trail, where he would suck a little harder for oxygen at higher altitude. Forget uphill transparency; I wanted some up-the-mountain justice. But that wasn't my mission. Nothing about that approach to confronting his inappropriate behavior would cause him to look uphill at me and grasp the higher set of personal values and character I offered him. Rats! This transparency thing is hard.

Are you beginning to sense how difficult it is to begin to correct jerks on the job by creating a transparent environment in which you represent a standard of responsible behavior? Full two-way transparency requires your willingness to endure the same conditions as everyone else in your work environment, yet rise above those conditions to represent an answer to those damaging it.

For me and my counselors, this involved a willingness to get wet, cold, and hot, have food stolen, be spat on by irate kids, tolerate painfully long problem-solving sessions, risk serious injury, and set aside personal needs for days at a time—all while carrying a backpack that proportionally weighed 50 percent more than the participants were asked to carry. That's leadership, the type you will need to muster, and that is what drove me to join the group that gathered beside the Mora River to address Beto's problem. Beto had to be shown an uphill view of someone whose values, beliefs, and mission in life are based on something other than where the hideous strength directs them. Your task at work is similar.

In the end, transparency is not a policy or a procedure; it's a personal choice you make.

Transparent Leadership

Few businesses build their business operations on the values of one man as closely as has Chick-fil-A. From the beginning of his business empire more than sixty years ago, the late S. Truett Cathy, founder of the Chick-fil-A restaurants, made the choice to be a transparent leader. You can't miss his imprint. Just try to purchase anything at a Chick-fil-A on Sunday. They are closed, the result of a faith-inspired business decision by Cathy.

Cathy's bold decision to allow his heart to influence his business decisions was derided by business experts. Since fast food restaurants typically earn 20 percent of their revenue from Sunday sales, he was told his business would fail if his restaurants did not open for Sunday business. Cathy called it "the best business decision I ever made." What he knew, and what business pundits failed to consider, was the potential for Chick-fil-A's success based on noneconomic factors, particularly the transfer of Cathy's personal values to his business organization. Closing its doors on Sunday is an example.

Being closed on Sundays "helps attract employees that appreciate having Sunday off," said Cathy. "It helps stabilize their family, too."[3] Savings in personnel turnover costs alone justify his decision. Most Chick-fil-A owner-operators have an amazingly low personnel turnover rate, annually under 5 percent—unheard of in the restaurant industry.

Cathy's standards of transparent leadership also pay off in the everyday world of employee management. If any Chick-fil-A employees want to know the personal values required of them at work or the proper way to act toward customers and coworkers, all they need to do is to recall Truett Cathy.

When asked how Cathy's values are passed down to his employees, Jeff White, the owner-operator of several Chick-fil-A restaurants, spoke of uphill transparency. "I have to be genuinely living those values," White said, "because I know that Truett talked a lot about doing what we say we're going to do." Then he added, "I know my people [employees] are watching me closely. I'll open a door for people and go by the tables and visit guests. They know what my priorities are." Uphill transparency couldn't be described better.

To match perception to reality, I asked one of White's restaurant managers to tell me the source of his employee management standards. If the concept of transparency works at Chick-fil-A, he would tell me something similar to what his boss said. "The value system that Truett incorporated into Chick-fil-A helps me manage employees by giving me a reference point. That would be where we start," he said. There you have it. The uniformity of the message rang true. Truett Cathy established the standard of behavioral values, which are then made transparent through the various levels of his organization as benchmarks for employee performance.

Stepping into a cold, wet group problem-solving session with Beto Martinez and his agitated campmates, I wondered if my resolve to be transparent with them would really work. I couldn't blink in front of my staff, especially Carol Smith, Beto's probation officer. I had practically guaranteed her that I could help her reach him.

For some, like Truett Cathy, steadfast transparent leadership comes naturally, as a force of personality. Others of us are more reluctant. We need a vehicle of opportunity to sweep us off our feet, thrusting us to the forefront of visibility, where we can influence others.

I never intended to be the director of a pioneer program of wilderness therapy for troubled youth. Confronting others wasn't my thing. Yet after completing an innocent graduate course in wilderness leadership, I was presented with the unexpected chance to be a "wilderness survival specialist" with one of the largest juvenile justice departments in the United States. What a job title, huh? And what a surprise. Suddenly I was Ron Newton, wilderness dude, a transparent beacon of values to the supposedly unredeemable. Who could pass that up?

Debbie Sardone knows this kind of feeling, except her vehicle of opportunity was self-created. Sardone is the owner of Buckets & Bows Maid Service, and she serves as the "Maid Service Business Coach" to others in her industry. While building a successful small business of thirty employees provided Sardone with a sense of self-fulfillment, the feeling wasn't satisfying enough for her. Burdened because several women who were her clients suffered from cancer, Sardone followed her heart and began using her company to deliver free housecleaning services for women undergoing cancer treatment. Paying maids out of her company's profit, Sardone says her compassion led her to offer the service. Her reasoning is simple: "If I can help someone who is hurting, particularly women, why wouldn't I?"

What Debbie Sardone never saw coming was how her small step of compassion affected not only her employees but also her industry, bringing a heightened awareness of professional purpose to a labor force generally regarded as unskilled second class. Asked if her cleaning technicians have caught her vision, Sardone said, "Definitely. It's given them a greater sense of pride. The effect is to elevate our field staff to a higher level of professionalism than they ever felt they would have in this type of job."

Encouraged by employee feedback and the participation of other cleaning companies, Sardone incorporated the Cleaning For A Reason Foundation to extend similar support across the nation. With 1,200 maid services on its membership roll as of 2015, the foundation has assisted more than 17,000 women nationwide, providing free cleaning services valued at over $5 million.

Sardone says the impact on employee morale in her business is "huge." "Our employee comments state that Cleaning For A Reason is the largest single factor which makes our employees glad to work for Buckets and Bows Maid Service." The opportunity to participate in such a noble cause has helped engender an employee retention rate that is two-thirds higher than the national average for her business sector. It also has contributed to a noticeable reduction in the need for the heavy-handed employee micromanagement common to service industries.[4]

More often than not, this is how the power of transparent values is ignited in the workplace. A leader, reluctant or otherwise, steps out and puts his or her personal values on the auction block of acceptability, hoping to exert influence in whatever limited form is applicable. Then the values take root, reaping rewards of positive employee behavior never dreamed. Truett Cathy did it with his first restaurant, started on a mere $10,600, most of which was borrowed. Debbie Sardone did it as a simple act of compassion. I did it, stepping into a world of wilderness therapy that hadn't yet been invented. And if you will do it within your sphere of work influence, you can provide an alternative to the hideous strength enabling jerks on the job.

It's All Downhill From Here

Standing beside the Mora River, I scrambled to think how I could make the campers' problem-solving meeting as short as possible. It appeared that Beto was my jerk on the job and a simple confession from him would be nice, followed by a disciplinary slap on the wrist from his peers.

Except for a few isolated insults, the group's initial onslaught of verbal invectives toward Beto waned as we gathered by the river to dispense justice and wisdom to him. Each member's face was essentially hidden by a large nylon rain poncho. Considering the dark sky, steady rain, stinking ponchos, and canopy of evergreen trees extending above the campers, the group resembled a crop of large mushrooms.

The one exception was Carol Smith. She had a sly grin on her face, the equivalent of a radiant face against the dreary day. Did she know something I didn't? Perhaps for her it was the excitement of finally being able to nail the one kid on her caseload who, more than others, flaunted his invincibility to her face. Whatever. I wasn't buying her enthusiasm.

Bridgette was allowed to speak first in the session, telling how she discovered the Pop-Tarts were missing and then catching Beto standing next to her backpack with crumbs and jelly all over his face. Nuff said.

Then it was Beto's turn. Would he yield to the transparent value of responsibility confronting him, or would he resist? I turned to him and asked his response to the young lady's accusation.

"I didn't do it," he replied, flashing his Teflon smile.

Say what?

"I didn't do it. And it's my word against hers," he repeated.

It may or may not have been a quirk of fate, but at that exact moment an ominous clap of thunder rolled down from the 12,000-foot peaks surrounding the mountain valley where Beto calmly stated his words of defiance.

Take note. The character-challenged individuals in your workplace will not yield easily to the values of personal maturity you represent. When I asked Roy Harbin of Graywater Marine if his volatile temperament may have contributed to the reluctance of his boat captains to report their barge grounding to him, he exploded, screaming at me. Then he enlisted his boss, himself a culpable adult brat, and they both verbally berated me. Adult brats do not react kindly to those who solicit the truth, so be patient.

A substantial increase in rain and wind appeared suddenly with the thunder, whipping about indiscriminately, lashing anything in its path. That, plus the audacity of Beto's denial, amplified the barrage of insults hurled his way. An impish smile was all that returned.

Beto had played this game before and won. I feared Carol Smith, standing three people to my left in our circle, was beginning to believe I had sold her a bill of goods about the power of transparent values. After *half an hour* standing in this ring of immovable humanity, I shot her a glance. She was rubbing her hands together, perhaps to keep them warm or maybe in preparation of wrapping them around my neck. I couldn't tell. When I finally made eye contact with her *an hour* into the session, her sly Mona Lisa smile told me I needn't worry. She was still waiting patiently for Beto's demise.

But *two hours* into the session, with cold rain continuing and hail beginning to descend over the mountain ridge toward us, I knew I needed to take action. By that time, the group had resigned itself to Beto's resistance and had stopped trying to solicit his confession. The hideous strength had won, so it seemed. The delinquents who had initially mustered a modicum of righteousness had now quietly retreated into their emotionally self-centered holes, their outrage quelled, content to let Beto get away with his self-destructive behavior.

Not wanting to disturb the group's near-comatose dynamics, I began to make my way toward Carol as unobtrusively as possible. Actually, I should say, like a big chicken I made my way toward Carol, slyly swapping places with the person to my left until I reached her. I had given up. The cold, rain, lightning, threat of hail, Beto's dogged resistance in light of his obvious guilt—all of it made me want to give up. No battle over values was worth it. I was going to quietly apologize to Carol, suggest we adjourn the session, and catch Beto in some other misdeed down the trail. Cluck, cluck.

Then as I leaned toward her to whisper my foolish plan, she beat me to it. "Oh boy," she said, rubbing her hands together in glee. "We've got him just where we want him, don't we? Look at him squirm. He's going to tell us the truth eventually."

"Yes, ma'am," I replied. "That's exactly what I was going to tell you." And with that bit of attitude correction, I spent the next several minutes slithering back to my original spot in the circle.

TRUTH FROM TRANSPARENCY

What a fortunate dope I considered myself. Carol Smith had set me straight before I self-destructed. Her encouragement reminded me of a valuable lesson I learned in graduate school but was prepared to ignore under the circumstances. (Hang with me here. I need to sound like an intellectual for a few seconds while I describe the lesson I almost threw away.)

In ancient times, the wisdom writers used a classical Hebrew word, *nakoach*, to describe today's concept of personal transparency. Our limited English translation for the word (we are so black and white) is most often "straightforward" or "clear." *Nakoach* is derived from a most delectable Hebrew root word that offers a bevy of flavors. Besides straightforward, it can also mean "to be in front of," "in the sight of," and "integrity," meaning plain, right, or upright.[5]

The wisdom I almost discarded is this: personal transparency will lead you to integrity, defined as "the quality of being honest and having strong moral principles, or moral uprightness." Transparency, particularly in regard to your values, is a moral issue. By thinking about walking away from the group session confronting Beto, I was considering doing the wrong thing. If I did that, I'd be no better than he. If you live by a proverbial sight-and-sound rule—be a leader out front, your values visible to all, risk being vulnerable—honesty will result. Truth will come to light.

Carol Smith knew this instinctively. She knew Beto was going to tell us the truth because a system of organizational transparency (the sight-and-sound rule) caught him in the act of stealing and a system of personal transparency (the group problem-solving session) was forcing him to tell the truth. For me to consider giving up that power, the power to find the truth, was a fundamental error on my part.

Don't be tempted to make the same mistake I almost made. Remember the lesson. Transparency and truth are indelibly linked. You rediscover the value of honesty, the kidnap victim of adult brats, through transparency.

TKO, Round 2

Fortified by Carol's resolve, I recommitted myself to seeking the truth from the handsome, likable fifteen-year-old with a mischievous smile and a tendency to lie like a politician. *Three hours* into the session, when we were nearly numb from having stood in the same place, hail descended on us. Perhaps God was going to get Beto before I did.

With the stinging hail came a renewed onslaught of insults toward not only Beto but me as well. Somehow I was perceived as an equal victimizer, and the kids let me know it. That stung more than the hail. Bowing my head half out of guilt and half to protect myself from the hail, I heard a voice say, "Okay, I admit it. I stole the Pop-Tarts." Looking toward Beto, I saw a young man step forward in the circle to again offer his confession. "I admit it," he said tearfully, but it wasn't Beto speaking. It was a kid named Victor. Surprise, surprise.

Victor Robinson was an innocent-looking fourteen-year-old who had fallen into trouble as the product of abusive, cocaine-addicted parents. A year earlier, Victor's older brother had participated on one of my trips, and I knew he had interceded on several occasions to protect Victor from parental abuse. Victor Robinson was a juvenile offender, but he also was a victim.

As soon as Victor stepped forward, Beto followed him, saying, "I stole the Pop-Tarts, too." When he did, the puzzle pieces encompassing the whole truth fit together.

Victor needed a surrogate brother to protect and provide for him. Beto needed to be accepted by others. The stressful wilderness experience had resulted in a bond of loyalty between the two that sealed as fast as contact cement. In criminal terms, Beto was guilty of fronting for Victor, carrying forth illegal activities that enabled Victor, his accomplice, to hide his deeper involvement from authorities. In street terms, it is called a gang.

Any possible exuberance to be gained from Beto's confession disappeared in light of Victor's participation. That's almost always how it is busting bad boys and adult brats. It's bittersweet. Part of it comes from discovering firsthand the extended impact of the hideous strength that leads them astray. Who would have thought that misplaced loyalty was a factor in Beto's theft or that two people were involved? Do you think you have one adult brat on the job? A handful? Look again.

Another part is the pure exhaustion you feel from keeping your guard up, from remaining vigilant in modeling your values to those who need to see them. It's like a heavyweight fight you must win by TKO—knockout by transparency. After the slugfest, you have no energy left to celebrate. You're too occupied recovering your faculties. Expect to feel confused.

THE QUESTION OF HOW

If you are convinced by now of the power of transparency to reveal truth—and I hope you are—then the immediate question you likely have is *how.* How do you go about integrating your personally transparent values into the fabric of your work environment so that you counter the undesirable behavior of jerks on the job? How do you raise the character bar so that adult brats are exposed and are forced to either change or leave? Maybe you can't take your boss, coworkers, employees, or contractor out on the camp trail to do a Beto-like job of "gotcha," but Art Rollins did.

Art, a multiple Purple Heart recipient from his military service in Vietnam, intuitively knew that a character-building experience comprised of tough times would not only allow him to expose his values to his employees but also would show him theirs. So off to the wilderness we went on a short expedition with all his senior truck drivers, including the deluded one who thought he could land a Boeing 747 better than an airplane pilot could drive his rig.

I wish you could have witnessed the group problem-solving session that developed on the second night of our trip. Emotions, stifled for years, came pouring forth. Tears from brawny truck drivers punctuated concerns over everything from complaints about fatigue on the job to company loyalty. Managers cried, too, over senseless irresponsible acts of behavior coming from employees they so dearly wanted to "grow up." By trip's end, there was no question as to the character strengths and weaknesses of each participant, including what they needed to do to meet Art's personal standards. The new group unity forged on the trip, born from transparency leading to truth, was worth every moment of temporary trauma on the trail. Even now, I can hear everyone singing the strains of "Puff the Magic Dragon" as we headed down the road back to civilization.

Still, unless you're the boss, you probably aren't in a position to command such a wilderness experience in your organization. How do you proceed?

Sorry, I can't tell you unless I know your specific situation. What I can do is share with you how some have begun the process in their workplace. You can draw courage and ideas from them, then follow the guidelines at the end of the chapter to develop your own plan:

- Bobby, a man of high moral standards, has few problems with the character of coworkers at his small engineering firm, but at one time he was constantly pressured by a client to accompany him to strip clubs whenever the client visited from out of town. In each incident, Bobby would try to subvert the client's plans by inventing bogus reasons to dine elsewhere. Eventually Bobby faced his client, stating that his life values precluded such activities. The client thanked Bobby and vowed to quit attending strip clubs himself. Bobby retained the client, increasing both his reputation and volume of business with the man.
- Gary is a safety supervisor on large-scale construction projects for a worldwide leader in his industry. He believes there is a direct link between the core values of safety and one's personal character. Gary was dismayed when project

managers on his job ignored obvious safety violations while inspecting the work of contractors. A few managers were openly arrogant in resisting Gary. To heighten exposure of his personal values and expectations to his project managers, Gary arranged for a short training session linking safety values to personal values. A value-based standard for safety inspections was then instituted, tying quality of safety observation to quality of personal character. Gary left his managers nowhere to hide other than behind their character deficit.

- Kathy manages a tax appraisal district and strongly believes her staff's effectiveness in appraising tax values is related to their ability to express genuine empathy to property owners. When two key members of her staff descended into an egocentric territorial squabble, Kathy's standard for empathy was cast aside. Not only was staff unity damaged, but property owners also received subpar service. Kathy shut down her team's operations for a day to hold a staff meeting in which she clearly defined empathy and empathetic behavior standards. One of her two adult brats resigned shortly afterward. The other called the meeting "eye-opening" and said, "I will try to be better at my job by understanding how property owners look at me and how I look at them."

Rule Of Thumb

In lieu of being able to speak directly to your specific work situation, here are four guidelines to help you develop adult brat-busting "truth from transparency" measures.

1. Carefully Consider the Values You Are Trying to Transparently Communicate

You should choose your battles well, focusing on specific values that are evident and measurable in the adult brats you are attempting to neutralize. Whereas honesty is the major value redeemed through transparency, you need to specifically define your value target by asking, "Honesty in what?" With Bobby, it was honesty in his moral stance on visiting strip clubs; Gary wanted honesty in protecting the lives of others; Kathy desired honesty in the expression of empathy. They each had a tangible standard.

2. Wage Your Battle against Specific Behaviors, Not the Entire Hideous Strength

Nothing will more quickly destroy your effort to confront adult brats through transparency than to be perceived as a wild-eyed moralizer who constantly screams about the generalized decay of values in society. You need to target specific behaviors of problematic employees in your workplace, not rail against them generally as if everything they do is of the devil. Beto was caught stealing, and his group session focused on that one act, not on the social factors that drove him to crime.

I offer arguments in this book about the collective effect of certain social factors on the general behavior of our society. The purpose of these arguments is to illustrate how adult brats are created and empowered, not how to confront and correct them. However true my arguments may be, please don't hit suspected adult brats over the head with them as a curative measure for their behavior.

3. Embody the Values You Want to Represent before Setting Yourself Up as an Example

I've already confessed how difficult it was for me to serve in a representative capacity, even though I was experienced in the role and I had the awesome wilderness learning environment as my ally. Transparent leaders are those who have followers. Before stepping out as a symbolic figure, ask yourself if anyone will follow you. Carol Smith was willing to follow my lead with Beto, but that's only because she spoke to me before I disqualified myself.

4. **Reconcile Your Method for Transparently Communicating Your Values with Your Business's Employee Management Policies and Practices**

In ridding your workplace of its crisis of character, make sure you don't become part of the problem instead of part of the cure. Violating your business's policies of employee management or abusing your position of influence over others may not only negate the transparency you aspire; it may hand a victory to your jerks on the job. Be an example to others beyond reproach (see preceding guideline) by following your organization's rules for employee engagement.

The Next Mountain

Haitians have a phrase that aptly describes the daily struggle to survive in their poverty-stricken country: "Behind the mountain there's another mountain." Life is not easy there.

In our journey to climb over the mountain range formed by the hideous strength, we've only climbed the peak of personal transparency, where we've found the lost value of honesty. As we look out from our lofty perch, we realize that where we stand is only one of several peaks to climb to reach our goal—winning the workplace battle against personal immaturity.

There's another peak immediately ahead, but it's higher than the one we are on. Gear up for another difficult climb.

Chapter Seven

Restoring Workplace Accountability

University of Miami psychology professor Michael McCullough, an expert on revenge and forgiveness, says, "The urge to take revenge or punish cheaters is not a disease or toxin or sign that something has gone wrong." Instead, he calls such instincts a natural solution.[1]

Professor McCullough could have drawn his conclusion from Bridgette Kleghorn, the camper most offended by Beto Martinez's theft of breakfast food. It was her backpack that Beto pilfered and her camp group he betrayed. With the group gathered by the Mora River, on the tail end of a bone-chilling three-hour tussle with Beto, the natural solution Bridgette offered for Beto and Victor's unfaithfulness was to hang the poor offenders. Revenge, in her mind, was best served fast.

Bridgette's suggestion was delivered with a serious tone of self-serving authority that life's vicissitudes had taught her to use well (as Beto used his smile), but I quickly let her know that hanging was out of the question. So were flogging, starvation, and abandonment, all of which she rapidly offered as alternatives. Discouraging these suggestions was easy; getting her group to think of constructive ways to help Beto and Victor learn to behave properly was difficult.

Having doused Bridgette's far-fetched punitive proposals in front of our shivering camp group, I applauded her dogged determination to hold the perpetrators liable for their disloyalty. She was thinking correctly, in part, by moving quickly past the stage of determining liability to the next stage of the group process, but her goal was wrong.

Punishment wasn't the primary purpose of the group meeting; it was to confront and correct the boys' improper behavior, specifically the *lack of self-discipline* that contributed to their disloyalty to the group.

Remember earlier, when we defined delinquency in terms of the lack of self-discipline that occurs when restraint isn't provided? Beto and Victor can serve as Exhibit A; they were youngsters, much like adult brats, who lacked what commentator Walter Lippmann describes as the support of a discipline that is rational and transcends their immediate promptings, enabling them to endure discomfort, pain, and danger.[2] On a lower level, the boys couldn't see past their stomachs.

If the group determined that discipline was to be included as some part of their correcting process, it was fine with me. But to automatically lump liability and punishment together, despite the natural instinct to do so, accomplishes little more than spanking a child without purpose. It only toughens the rear end; it doesn't teach the child. Beto and Victor needed teaching as well as some toughening.

Despite her misguided motive, the fact that Bridgette was using the second rule of the trail to achieve anything was encouraging. Some kids might have simply exercised a lack of self-discipline of their own, slugging Beto when they initially saw the crumbs on his face. At least she was using the system of rules we had established for her—guidelines that can be adapted to hold undisciplined, disloyal adult brats accountable in your workplace.

Rule 2: Huddle-Ups

The huddle-up rule: *You must come immediately to all huddle-ups when they are called, regardless of when they are called or for what purpose, and you must participate in the huddle-up until the purpose of the huddle-up is realized.*

Huddle-up. That's the name for the group problem-solving session that hounded Beto and Victor for three hours, driving them to accountability. In camp vernacular, a huddle-up is little more than a circle in which everyone in a group must stand until the purpose of the huddle-up is addressed. Under Rule 2, leaving a huddle-up is not an option. This explains why no one quit when Beto's huddle-up slogged into oblivion. (I'm obviously overlooking my momentary point of weakness here.)

The basic concept of using peer pressure to solve problems of personal responsibility isn't new. In the 1940s, Campbell Loughmiller adopted a huddle-up system for use in his Salesmanship Club Camp for emotionally troubled children. Much earlier, Inuit tribe members, living in remote societies without institutional law, developed a practice of shouting group disapproval at someone caught stealing or cheating. After witnessing an Inuit shouting ceremony, anthropologist Edie Turner described the shout as more like a blast. "The one time I witnessed an Inuit woman do this to someone," she said, "the blast practically ricocheted off of me."[3]

The blast I felt from Bridgette after denying her punitive proposals was the flash of her icy stare. Her eyes told me, "Duh. Why in the world did you lead me down this three-hour torture trail if you aren't going to let me kill my prey? What good is the huddle-up rule if it doesn't deliver on its promise?"

Poor girl. She wanted desperately for someone to be punished. Burned by disloyalty, she wanted to eliminate her enemies, not reach out to them and help them achieve self-discipline. Her answer to disloyalty was more disloyalty—alienating the perpetrators through excessive punishment. But such an attitude would get her and our group nowhere up the trail to helping Beto and Victor develop self-discipline.

Feeling Like A Business Bridgette

Don't tell me that you haven't experienced Bridgette's gut feeling about some adult brat in your workplace. At one point, you've probably felt like calling a huddle-up, pointing a finger of responsibility, and pulling the trigger of punishment on somebody you think had betrayed you or your organization—if only you could. I know that's how George Ritter felt when I saw him standing in a corner after church one Sunday, arms folded, brow furrowed, with pain written on his face. The look was unmistakably Bridgettesque.

George is a senior executive with one of the eleven businesses highlighted in Jim Collins's best-selling book *Good to Great*,[4] meaning that George works for a company that Collins thinks has elevated its status from a good company to a great one, clearly superior to its competitors. In the case of George's company, a significant part of its superiority was rooted in the company's irrevocable loyalty to its employees.

Notice I said *was* rooted in the company's irrevocable loyalty to its employees. That was before the Sunday morning when George told me a bitter story of betrayal that literally made him ill.

According to George, for the first time in his company's history, the decision had been made to "right-size" the organization by outsourcing labor. While the number of workers losing their jobs was a mere fraction of the company's employees, the groundwork for additional layoffs of once-important corporate family members had been established.

Several factors played into the company's decision to turn its back on the great value of loyalty. Foremost was the increased use of economic projection models that depend heavily on project management rather than on people for their success.

Commenting on the repressed face of economists who build and use similar economic models to manage investments, columnist David Brooks of the *New York Times* said, "But many economists are trained to downplay emotion, social psychology and moral norms, and so produce bloodless and incomplete descriptions of what's going on. The truth is, decision-making is an inherently emotional process."[5]

George Ritter's assessment was more blunt. "We've exchanged leadership for project management," he said. "Used to be, the ability to lead and develop people was the mark of a successful manager." Since his company felt it could purchase project management talent from outside the organization, commitment to the development of its own leaders was no longer necessary. They became expendable, and the value of loyalty to employees became what George called a "dinosaur value"—extinct.

To sugarcoat the betrayal, George said, the employment terminology used by his company had changed, making the policy change sound innocuous, even beneficial to employees. A new contract with employees was announced, in which they were "free" to explore employment with other companies, and of course, the company was free to hire from outside its current labor pool. Disloyalty on all levels was invited, particularly if the replacement price tag was lower than the original one.

The result, said George, is that his company's "employees are now viewed as interchangeable, possessing completely transferable skill sets.

"The trend," he continued, "is to exchange the loyal employee for the mercenary."

All this weighed on George Ritter that Sunday morning, making him angry. He wanted a huddle-up with those he knew to be the perpetrators—adult brats, if you will—of his company's unwise policy change, and he wanted them to admit their responsibility and be punished. But, he told me after calming down, that would be a waste of time. There's a greater purpose to accountability than simple punishment, he said.

Finding Real Accountability

George Ritter is right. Seeking revenge through the punishment of adult brats in your workplace may be personally satisfying, but it is a weak substitute for using the power of accountability to effectively combat the influence adult brats have on your business.

True, I could have settled for allowing Bridgette and her group to slap some heinous punishment on Beto and Victor, but what good would it have done in the long run? I've already told you that delinquents are emotionally insulated from the influence of punishment, and they are comfortable in dealing with self-defeating behaviors for which they are routinely punished. For some, punishment is a crown of achievement. The same is true for adult brat workers you may know. Punishment won't deter them or turn them around; it will even invigorate some.

That's the problem with the exercise of *external accountability,* "external" meaning me (or my peer group) forcing someone with unacceptable behavior to admit responsibility. It almost always leads to a punitive solution that is least likely to correct the undesirable behavior.

I'm not saying that external accountability isn't necessary. That's why we have rules, laws, regulations, policies, and such, and it's why my camp program used huddle-ups. But external accountability doesn't correct adult brat behavior; it only reveals it.

Think of external accountability in terms of a police officer who catches someone in the act of committing a traffic violation. The officer's job isn't to correct the driver's inappropriate behavior by teaching him better skills; it is to issue the driver a ticket that holds him accountable for his actions. The bad driver's behavior may improve for a short time simply because he was caught, but eventually he'll return to old habits. His behavior isn't corrected, merely cited.

To ultimately win the war against adult brats, you need to balance the trappings of external accountability with the power of *personal accountability.*

To describe personal accountability, the Greeks used the word *hupodikos*. Composed of two words, *hupo* (under) and *dike* (judicial decision or sentence), hupodikos is a personal reminder to us that we are to conduct ourselves as if we owe a legal obligation to authority and are already under some form of legal sentence. As such, we are liable for acting as authority would have us act, under authority's limitation.

Believe it or not, this constraint of personal accountability provides happiness. Or as Walter Lippmann said, we become happy by living within a system that restrains us and gives coherence to our desires. Have you noticed that adult brats never seem to be happy? That's because they lack the self-discipline needed to reach this degree of accountable living.

The power of personal accountability—behaving as if you are under obligation to authority—is equal to the power of transparency in modeling life-changing values to those who need them. That's why it was important for me to not let Bridgette step outside the bounds of acceptable conduct to punish Beto and Victor, and that's why George Ritter's initial thinking was also wrong. To deal with adult brats, you can't ignore personal accountability in the pursuit of punitive external accountability. If you do, they win.

Once Bridgette got that message in Beto's huddle-up, she began asking the right questions and making productive suggestions. "Okay," she asked, "what will you allow us to do in order to help the poor darlings learn their lesson?" Despite the sarcasm, she was on the right track. She was willing to help, within the bounds of acceptable behavior, to bring Beto and Victor into a loyal, beneficial relationship with the group. In the process, she was committing herself to be personally accountable to whatever reasonable plan of discipline I suggested.

In short, you can devise all the clever accountability traps (external accountability) you want to catch adult brats in your workplace, but capitalizing on them to create an adult brat-free environment is a matter of your willingness to exercise personal accountability.

I know it's hard to turn your back on the urge to settle the score with adult brats. As a proverbial mountain peak to scale on your way to eliminating their influence in your workplace, substituting personal accountability for revenge is one of the hardest peaks to climb.

But if you will allow your adult brats to witness your submission to authority—your personal obligation—you'll not only get your Beto and Victor immediately; in the long run you'll get your Bridgette, too. Furthermore, you'll discover a principle essential to dealing with adult brats, a truth that Bridgette taught me, like Carol Smith did, in a moment of weakness.

To show you this truth, I need to take you into the wilderness again, on a day when I wanted to throw Bridgette over a cliff. When we come back from the cliff's edge, I'll tell you how the lessons she taught me in this real-life adventure helped me save a client from the adult brats in its business.

THE LIMIT OF EXTERNAL ACCOUNTABILITY

At the conclusion of Beto's huddle-up, the focus of the camp group shifted from punishment to problem solving. Seizing on Bridgette's willingness to be personally accountable in helping bring Beto and Victor back into the fold, I gave her a minor assignment. She was to monitor any personal contact between the two and alert the group when the wannabe gang members seemed to be getting too chummy.

Over the next few days of hiking, Bridgette slowly warmed to her responsibility, but the effort wasn't without struggle. Several times I caught her reverting to her vengeful instinct, lording her position of minor authority over the poor boys, bossing them around. Each of her aggressive acts resulted in a huddle-up, with Bridgette vowing to do better, but we could never get her to stop calling Beto a "twerp."

Bridgette's probation officer told me that she would be open and easy to get along with. He lied. Bridgette was a fiery redhead, complex, confusing, manipulative, and Scarlett Johansson beautiful. It didn't help that she could rightly be described as statuesque—an advantage she used over Beto and Victor. They were a year younger than Bridgette and two years behind her in physical development. When she yelled "jump," they asked how high.

I knew Bridgette's history of multiple sexual abuse—she was the victim of both her biological father and a foster parent. One result of the abuse was her resistance to strong male leadership, explaining why Bridgette took every opportunity to yank the chain of authority on Beto and Victor. She wasn't after them; she was after me, or what I represented. If she could aggravate me by abusing whatever bit of personal responsibility I had given her over the boys, she would use the opportunity. Hers was a classic case of the passive-aggressive behavior I defined earlier, one of the behavioral earmarks of an adult brat at work.

Bridgette illustrates the limited effectiveness of external accountability to correct adult brat behavior. When adult brat workers are exposed and disciplined through the best "mousetrap" of accountability mechanisms—employee code of conduct, ethics standard, surveillance devices, or whatever—they often remain defiant. They simply shift their destructive behavior pattern from active (open) aggression to the more irritable passive mode.

In reaction to Bridgette's pitched battle against me, I asked Carol Smith and another female counselor to concentrate on holding Bridgette accountable. To their chagrin, she treated them with equal defiance, improving little as the trip progressed. The maturing power of personal accountability apparently wasn't working on Bridgette, at least not in the short term.

But I had the long term on my side. I knew that the tenor of our camping trip was about to radically change. Our first few days of hiking would end at a beautiful high mountain valley, accessible only by rappelling down a seventy-five-foot rock face. Think of it as the mother of all external accountability traps—a time and place where Bridgette *had* to be personally accountable for her behavior. Would she comply with my instructions as her rappelling instructor, living up to her responsibility to lower herself over the cliff to join her teammates below?

Finding Another Lost Value

"No! No! No! I don't want to go. You can't make me go. You . . . can't . . . make . . . me . . . go!" This is the sanitized version of Bridgette's first reaction to the seventy-five-foot descent awaiting her, shouted while she was still thirty feet from the rock's edge. No amount of persuasion could get her to come any closer, if only to form a realistic opinion of the challenge that awaited her. Neither could she see the absolute blast her campmates had as they each took their turn descending to the valley floor. So much for my hope that she would peacefully exercise some personal responsibility.

Rappelling is virtually all a mind game. Gravity does the work; all the rappeller does is make the decision to lean backward over the rock edge, move her feet down the rock face, and determine how fast she wants to travel. Oh, and she must *trust* the person who sets up the rappelling gear, hooks her into the harness, and talks her into leaning out into thin air. In this case, me.

Trust? I would have settled for a moment of silence so I could calmly talk to her. But she would not open the door for me to explain anything to her, least of all why she should trust me and fulfill her obligation to the camp group. Instead, more invectives followed—loud ones—while I stood thirty feet from her, waiting for her to give me any sign that she was willing to cooperate. None came.

Stop me if you've heard this one before. Fifteen minutes turned into thirty; thirty into almost an hour. It was like Beto and his huddle-up all over again, except this time there was no huddle-up, just a one-on-one battle about personal accountability.

Finally, my patience wearing thin, I raised the level of my voice and began to speak in a commanding tone. "Bridgette, it's time. Stop your whining and come here." Amazingly, she responded, slowly moving toward me. Was I winning, or—given her background of abuse—had I simply become another abuser in her mind? I don't mind telling you, I felt horribly guilty at the time.

Having coached many employees in the skill of adult brat busting, I can say that the one point in the process that always gives pause is the very point I'm describing right now. Stepping forward among your peers to fulfill your obligation to personal accountability, despite what they may think of you, is nerve-racking. Holding others to their obligation can be downright intimidating.

Research on revenge and forgiveness indicates that we're basically a bunch of chickens when it comes to confronting coworkers, preferring to leave the hard work of enforcement to others. But in the same way we talked about leaders being willing to exercise the uncomfortable power of transparency, you need to be resolute in pursuit of accountability.

It appeared my perseverance with Bridgette was paying off as she slowly inched her way to me. Finally, I was able to assist her in putting on her harness, even drawing a weak laugh when I told her it could hold the weight of a Volkswagen. After hooking Bridgette into the rappel rope, I gradually led her to the rock's edge, where it started all over again.

"No! No! I don't want to go. You can't make me go. You . . . can't . . . make . . . me . . . go!" The victory that seemed so near disappeared in another round of defiant screams and cries. Once again time stood still as I waited for Bridgette. Fifteen, then twenty minutes—an eternity of emotional agony.

By then it was late afternoon, and mountain showers were threatening to cut short our long summer day. It was crucial to get everyone down in the valley and set up camp. Under the influence of Bridgette's stubbornness, the immense guilt I felt, and the imposing weather, I reached a breaking point. Speaking in a blunt, commanding tone, I ordered Bridgette to rappel down the cliff, telling her it would be easy. The feedback I received was instant, but it didn't come from Bridgette. It was from another camper.

"If it's so easy, Mr. Big Shot, why don't you do it?" she said.

"Thank you. I think I will," I replied. Then, turning to Bridgette, I asked her to rappel with me side by side, telling her that she could reach out and hold my hand if needed. Would she do it if I descended with her?

"Yes," she said.

Relinquishing my remaining instructor duties to one of my staff, I quickly grabbed an extra rope, tied it around a sturdy Douglas fir, and launched it over the rock face. Hooking myself into it, I stood by Bridgette as she again began to softly cry. "Let's go," I said.

Inch by inch, we backed toward the edge as I gave quiet instructions designed to promote confidence and calm. As we reached the precipice and our upper bodies leaned out over thin air, she never flinched.

Over the edge we went, slowly, until we felt the security that comes with a tight rappel rope and a harness that works. The rest would be downhill, literally.

Progressing past the ten-foot mark, I took a moment to look down at the campers gathered below, then out over the mountain valley. Then my eye caught the blur of something coming at me from Bridgette's way. Startled, I swung my head around and discovered it was Bridgette's left hand, held out for mine.

I took it.

In that moment I felt the euphoria of the breakthrough, but surprisingly the guilt remained. I had caused this young woman to scream and cry, to dig deep into the pits of her life and confront emotions long dormant, and to feel the intense pain that often accompanies the obligation of accountability. In return, she had taken a gigantic step toward avoiding adult brathood.

As we reached the bottom, Bridgette collapsed into my arms as she sobbed agonizingly, mixing her tears with the words I least expected to hear at the moment: "Thank you."

Thank you? I was stupid for not understanding what she was desperately trying to tell me on top of the cliff. *If you want my loyalty,* she was saying as best she could, *be an accountability partner with me, not someone who prods me into it. Show me your personal accountability, hold me to my obligations, and I will follow you.*

I was the one who should have thanked her, because the simple and priceless lesson she taught me is this: in the mountain you face with adult brats, loyalty—more than you ever imagined—can be found through holding people accountable.

BRIDGETTE MEETS BILLY, BILLY'S BOSS, AND BILLY'S BOSS'S BOSS

I hear you thinking (particularly if you are a guy), *Man, what a sappy story.* If you eat lightbulbs for fun, you might be asking, What has Bridgette's little pity party got to do with the real business world? *I may have a few adult brats in my workplace, but, come on, none of that melodramatic stuff about emotions and accountability exists in my work area.*

Perhaps. Then again, some emotional identification with my earlier story about Billy Taylor's struggles with his boss, Jake Nyland, caused you to pack your bag and travel with me on this journey. So let's explore Billy's story to its end, just as it happened in the real business world. Then you can tell me if Bridgette's story belongs to the big boys of business. My guess is that you'll see a lot more of Bridgette and her campmates in Billy's workplace—and yours—than you care to admit.

If you remember Billy, he was the new hire lab technician I attempted to interview while visiting a client's job site (chapter 1). I was there to investigate the low employee morale and excessive personnel turnover rate occurring in Billy's business unit, a small service center of twelve employees that is part of a large communications company.

Billy was a factory-trained bench technician who loved to repair two-way radios and radio systems. Unfortunately for Billy, his foreman-level supervisor, Jake, was a blabbermouth adult brat.

Do you remember Billy's reaction to Jake's incessant self-aggrandizement? Pointing to Jake, Billy asked me, "Am I going to turn out to be like him?"

Here's the rest of what Billy said after asking his perceptive question. "Because if I'm going to turn out to be like him, I'll quit this job right now. I don't want to be married to this job like Jake, allowing it to ruin my life. I've got too much else to live for."

Billy then pulled out his wallet, showing me a picture of his wife and their young child. In the compartment next to the picture was Billy's bench technician certification card, which he pointed to with pride. He also showed me other professional certifications he had earned. No doubt there was a bit of self-centered Generation Me in Billy, but it wasn't the type of delusional self-importance that marks much of his age group. Billy was the real deal, an accountable man of character.

Because of his integrity, Billy's insinuation that Jake had a negative effect on employee engagement concerned me. Following the chain of command, I decided to look uphill from Jake (remember uphill transparency?) to see if I could find the genesis of Jake's warped sense of loyalty.

As Mark Miller, vice president of training and development for Chick-fil-A told me, "All value systems are transparent. They may not be cohesive or aligned, but if you stay in an organization for about 24 hours, you'll know what its value system is."

It took less than twenty-four hours to interview and observe the three managers above Jake's level. By the time I finished, *cohesive* and *aligned* were the least applicable terms I found to describe the value of loyalty in Billy's business unit. Instead, I found something that would make Bridgette and Beto feel right at home.

Thomas Whiteside was the business unit's senior manager. Called Captain Whitey by his employees because they couldn't call him Captain Bligh to his face, Whiteside was a humorless man of rigid habits. When I attempted to sit in a comfortable-looking chair at the snack room dining table, I was told by Jake that it was Captain Whitey's chair and I couldn't sit in it. Why I couldn't sit in Whitey's chair in his absence puzzled me. Perhaps Whitey was afraid someone would mess up the butt prints he'd left in the chair during his twenty-two-year reign as the unit's manager.

In keeping with his captain's persona, Whitey boasted that he ran a stern ship, tolerating no guff from employees. Pointing his finger in my face, he stated as fact, "You won't find any problems in my business unit." From both his statement and his intimidating posture, I interpreted his words as a mild warning. *Get off my boat.*

When I asked him why his business unit had such high personnel turnover rates, he blamed it on the "damn kids" his company hired. They didn't have any work ethic and always wanted to know, "What's in it for me?" He then singled out Jake as the only employee who was worth a flip.

In contrast to Whitey, the unit's chief technical manager, Todd Patterson, was a friendly codger who loved to meander around the repair shop's workstations, visiting at length with all the employees except Jake. During lunch break, after Whitey went back to work, Todd would engage two of his favorite employees in a quick game of cards. I initially thought the camaraderie established by Todd was commendable, but that was before I met Jeff Simmons, the unit's assistant manager.

Jeff was an apprehensive thirty-something whose anxiety stemmed from Jake's footprints on his back, placed there by Jake's frequent circumventing of the chain of command. His eyes searching to ensure that no one was listening in, Jeff whispered to me that Jake had no hesitation about appealing directly to Whitey. The two were so much alike, he said, it was scary.

Still, for a man who thought he mattered little in the hierarchy, Jeff's positive influence on nearly all the employees was evident. One after another, they told me that Jeff was a great sounding board for their frustrations with both Jake's and Whitey's authoritarian micromanagement. They also mentioned something else— they were tired of being pulled between Whitey and Todd.

After I gained Jeff's confidence, I asked him why the employees would feel torn between Whitey and Todd. The story he told me explained a lot.

Whitey and Todd had both entered employment with the company at the same time, having been best of friends. As both rose through the ranks, the competition between them increased, culminating in an incident twenty-three years before in which Todd accused Whitey of cheating the company out of thirty-four dollars in petty cash. Todd's accusation was never substantiated, and soon afterward Whitey received a promotion to the unit manager's position. Since that time, the two had rarely spoken to each other.

Twenty-two years of silence ensued between two men, both managers, working in the same small business unit. That's hard to do, simply from a logistical viewpoint. Take into consideration that the business unit had been sold to new owners on three occasions during the past quarter century. That's three new senior managers from some corporate office who supposedly knew about the feud but did nothing about it. The mere existence of such a long-running conflict is astounding.

Keep in mind also that this is not Graywater Marine I'm talking about. There was no backwater mentality of fistfights and irresistible corporate edicts involved here. This was a small unit of a modern communications company doing business in the eighth largest urban area of the United States. And what they had in their workplace was a culture of employee loyalty divided between managerial personalities, the unchecked result of which was a bleeding pocketbook of personnel turnover costs. Personal accountability to the company had become personal accountability to one of two people, either Whitey or Todd.

What they really had was a Bridgette, a Beto, and a Victor, failing their obligation to be accountable to a greater cause than themselves, pretending to serve an organization that failed to provide them external accountability.

This group needed a huddle-up—big time. And that's exactly what I gave it.

Shoot-Out At The Not-So-Okay Corral

So, how did Captain Whitey react to my suggestion to call a staff meeting for the purpose of addressing his conflict with Todd and correcting any accountability issues harmful to the organization? "No! No! You can't make me go. You . . . can't . . . make . . . me . . . go!"

Perhaps it wasn't that bad, but it did involve an attempt to threaten me into dropping the idea. Bridgette pitched a fit; Beto stonewalled; Whitey bullied. Be prepared. Just like delinquents, adult brats don't cotton to accountability.

Once Whitey realized I wouldn't relent (consultants working under the mandate of upper management can have such sweet power), he immediately called all his staff to the snack room. Huffing and puffing as if mortally wounded, he didn't wait for any democratic group process to begin. It was more like Guantanamo Bay.

Walking up to each nonmanagement employee except Jake, Whitey pointed his finger in each face, demanding to know who had anything bad to say about him. In the process, he called in every guilt-laden loyalty marker he could.

"By God," he said to one employee, "your father and I worked together here years ago. A great man he was, too. When he asked me to get you a job here, I did. Now, what do you have to say about what Newton is telling me?"

Just like Bridgette had done, Whitey framed his struggle against accountability as a battle against Ron Newton. Psychologists call this *transference*, or a redirection of feeling. It's a frequently used tactic to divert responsibility away from oneself. Just think of O. J.'s "dream team" of defense lawyers; they didn't defend O. J. as much as they prosecuted the Los Angeles police department.

Whitey's employees reacted as you might expect for a group under such pressure from its autocratic leader. Silence. Not a word. Eyes cast down. I was hung out to dry, along with any support for personal accountability.

Seizing on the pause, I began to conduct the group more like a problem-solving session than the Spanish Inquisition. Calmly putting forth the conclusions I had reached, I asked the group if anyone wished to comment. It was time for the group to acknowledge the truth that was transparent to all.

More agonizing silence followed. You could hear Whitey's mental laughter as he sensed victory over those he thought were gutless, not worthy of his respect.

Then, as with Victor Robinson, a nervous voice spoke up and set accountability in motion.

"Whitey, I think there's a lot of truth to what Ron is saying." It was Jeff, and with his words, the real leader of the group emerged.

With Jeff demonstrating his personal accountability, others followed. In rapid succession, employee after employee stepped forward, reciting multiple incidents of Whitey's adult brat behavior. They spoke of workers who decided to leave the company rather than put up with Todd and Whitey's petty game of dividing and demanding the loyalty of employees, and they blamed Whitey for allowing Jake's unchecked nauseous behavior. Even Billy, the rookie, spoke out. In the end, the body of evidence presented by the group left Whitey, Todd, and Jake speechless.

Loyalty—true loyalty—blossomed in the process. The whole group, except for the adult brats exposed in the meeting, left the room with a tremendous sense of pride and an equally large feeling of relief.

I can't say that Whitey cried in my arms and told me "Thank you" like Bridgette did after her rappel. Shucks. But for both him and Bridgette, a new trail was opened. Bridgette continued along her new pathway toward character growth, becoming less manipulative and defensive as her trip progressed. Beto became like a little brother to her, and I ceased to be her enemy.

Whitey's fate was different. With both transparency and liability exposing the truth about him, his employees began to divulge to me the depths of his abusive ways. Soon after the staff meeting was adjourned, his demure administrative assistant told me that Whitey had been harassing her for several years, despite her protests. She had retained an attorney but had resisted taking any legal action because she was afraid of losing her job.

I immediately reported my findings to the company. Based on their investigation, Whitey was terminated from employment.

In his place, Jeff was promoted. Under his guidance, a focus on building employee loyalty through shared accountability developed, convincing Billy not to leave the company. Jake, his supervisor, made the opposite decision.

As for Todd, in the absence of his longtime nemesis, work was no fun. What good is it if there is no pot to stir? Todd retired a few months after Whitey was fired, leaving Jeff with an adult brat-free workplace. Accountability works; loyalty follows.

A WORKPLACE WITHOUT HUDDLE-UPS

You may work in an organization where bold moves like a huddle-up may not be encouraged or may not even be feasible. Don't worry. I'm not suggesting you conduct actual huddle-ups.

I remember naively thinking how organized huddle-ups would be a great employee management tool for Art Rollins's truckers. What did I know? I was straight out of the woods. So I developed what I felt was a workable business model for using huddle-ups, even calling them by that name. The idea flopped. Nothing is as deflating as hearing your prize problem-solving tool called a "cuddle-up" by big, burly truckers.

Whenever possible, though, you need to practice in an *organized manner* the principles of transparency and accountability. They are essential to combating the pseudoloyalty perpetrated by adult brats. In whatever form you are allowed to exercise both external and personal accountability in your work environment, here are five key points you should remember.

1. The Accountability Process Begins with You

Think of the formula for accountability success this way: it's 10 percent external accountability combined with 90 percent personal accountability.

The problem with waiting for external accountability traps to work is that, by definition, accountability is your obligation, not someone else's. If you want to hold adult brats accountable, you are responsible for 90 percent of the initiation process. It all begins with raising the bar of expectation for yourself so that others may see and follow your example.

2. Confronting Adult Brats in Your Work Area Is Something You Can Do inside Your Sphere of Influence

You should always assume that the fight against adult brats in your area of work influence is your battle. If you are an employee in a mid- to large-size business, don't expect your employee management bureaucracy to come to your rescue and hold adult brats accountable for you. If you work in a small business, don't feel that you are too close to the situation to take action.

The consistency of contact you have with adult brats in your work area should determine your involvement. Do you routinely interact with adult brats at work? Then they are within your sphere of influence. Go get 'em.

3. Develop Thick Skin because Initially You Will Not Be Popular

Sharp verbal feedback from campers and threatening postures from business managers are only a few of the slings and arrows I've faced in confronting and correcting the character of others. Although your colleagues may express their initial displeasure to you differently, you should expect similar feedback when you rock the boat to rid your workplace of adult brats.

Do not expect everyone of sound character to initially be fighting by your side. Most people like to avoid conflict or controversy.

Gradually, though, as loyalty is wrestled away from adult brats, others will join your effort.

You should mentally prepare yourself for this temporary unpopularity. Focusing on the long-term good of your leadership will help you endure short-term discomfort.

4. Make Sure the "Cure" of Accountability Is Not Worse than Its Cause

As I exhorted you in modeling the transparency of your personal values, so I encourage you to do the same with accountability. Make sure that whatever actions you take to externally trap adult brats or to model your personal accountability are within the guidelines of your company's employee management policies or operating procedures. Like Bridgette, you are not allowed to hang, flog, starve, or torture adult brats into renouncing their immature ways.

Remember, the purpose of accountability is not punishment or revenge; it's eliminating the influence of bad behavior. With adult brats, that means focusing accountability on helping them build self-discipline. If this involves disciplining employees or providing additional structure to their behavioral parameters, such measures need to be administered within the acceptable limits of your company's policies.

5. Build toward a "Critical Mass" That Convinces Adult Brats the Battle Is over and the Good Guys Have Won

Jeff and Billy were on my side in opposing Whitey and Jake. So were several other employees. Although Jeff initially opposed my confronting Whitey, he joined my effort as the staff meeting progressed. A critical mass of similar minds soon developed—critical in the sense that Whitey could not overcome it or deny its presence.

You are not alone in your opposition to adult brats in your workplace. Others will join you in your bravery if you will only step out and lead.

Knowing When You're Winning

I admit that it's somewhat unfair to give you an example like Whitey's staff meeting to illustrate how the accountability battle against adult brats is won. Such battles are not typically won that quickly, nor are they fought with the assistance of a consultant. Similarly, a three-hour huddle-up or rappel may portray the intense emotional turmoil you will feel as you stand up for values and responsibility, but stories on paper pass too quickly to convey the agonizing feeling of slow motion that accompanies the real thing in your workplace.

What you really want to know is two things: *How long will it take to win the battle?* and *How will I know I'm winning?*

I can't tell you how long it will take. That depends on too many variables unique to your situation. It could be over as amazingly fast as my experience with Whitey's business unit—about one week. Or it could drag on for months. I'm sorry I can't be more specific.

As for knowing when you are winning, two markers will help you know when the tide has turned in your favor.

First, look for what outsiders to your area of operation say about your work environment. If they notice that you've succeeded in establishing an adult brat-free zone, they'll let you know it in two ways. They'll either want to transfer to your department (in large companies) or beat a path to your door for employment. By the way, new hires, like Billy, are excellent sources of fresh perspective on how you're doing in winning the battle.

Second, when adult brats begin to change their tune, voicing their support for responsible behavior, you're winning. I clearly recall the day after Beto's huddle-up because it was such a defining moment. A huddle-up was called on another of the group members, someone who attempted to get away with a stunt just as foolish as Beto's. Less than five minutes into the huddle-up, Beto told the offending party, "You might as well tell them the truth; they're going to find out anyway." When you start getting that type of input, you're winning.

Preparing for the Hardest Step

I hear you breathing hard. This has been a hard mountain to climb. Between Mount Transparency and Mount Accountability, you've conquered two amazing peaks. They're the highest you'll climb on the journey to ridding your workplace of adult brats, but they're not the most difficult to climb. That's reserved for the other mountain you must tackle before your journey is over. Don't get cocky just yet.

For now, let's stop and eat some granola. You're probably hungry, and you'll definitely need the energy. The heart exercise required to conquer the next mountain makes everything you've done thus far look easy. Honesty and loyalty were surface finds compared with the depth you will need to dig to recover the next stolen value: compassion. The hideous strength has hidden it on a mountain in a place where few dare to tread.

Chapter Eight

Teaching Corruption-Busting Compassion

Dock foreman Ray Barnes is a mentally stable man. It says so on his job description: "A dock foreman must be stable under pressure, able to withstand the stress associated with the job, including discomfort, unpredictable weather, and potentially hazardous situations."

Nowhere does it mention he must also be able to cope with a couple of adult brat bosses whose concern for his emotional well-being borders on blatant neglect. But that's exactly what Ray was asked to do.

RAY

I met Ray when he worked at a grain storage terminal in the Midwest—the breadbasket of the United States. One of his primary duties was to oversee the loading and offloading of grain shipments at the terminal. His job required him to periodically stay long hours on the job site, particularly during harvest season when the high volume of shipments demanded his constant attention. It was not unusual for Ray to be away from home for forty-eight hours or more at a stretch. As Ray told me when he pointed to a truck waiting in line to unload, "I know who's boss here. It's those people."

During our conversation, several trucks arrived for offloading, providing a perfect opportunity to observe Ray as he assisted two other workers in the cumbersome unloading process. Despite his heavy workload, Ray was a gracious host, taking time to show me the measures involved in safely transferring the grain from truck to silo.

It was easy to like Ray. A personal warmth exuded from him that I have found is unusual for someone who works in the tough, impersonal environment of shipping and storage. Most dock foremen who spend years working with prickly truckers and cantankerous farmers end up a bit prickly themselves. Not Ray. Despite his twenty years of experience, the forty-year-old remained optimistic. He loved his job, his coworkers, his family, and his church. Ray was no adult brat.

After observing Ray and his crew for several hours, I returned to the terminal office to visit with the facility's general manager. Ray's immediate supervisor, the terminal's young operations manager, joined us in the discussion. Both were as nice as could be expected for managers who were forced by their home office to entertain me, but our polite chitchat revealed nothing of significance to my mission. I was there to investigate why the facility had recently experienced three lost-time accidents, one involving a leg that had been broken in six places.

Using Frank Bird's loss causation model (described in chapter 4) as a guide, I then asked the managers a series of deeper, probative questions to discover any root causes that may have contributed to the injuries. They freely answered each query concerning the company's job and system factors, frequently referencing the company's operations manual. But when I asked questions designed to reveal any personal factors, both men quickly clammed up, withdrawing into an emotionally empty bunker that would have delighted Richard Nixon. If any clues to the injuries were linked to the personal behavior of the two men, it was going to be next to impossible to find them.

I needed something to pry these men out of their emotional fortresses and give me insight into their character. It arrived in the form of a tragic telephone call to the office. The call was for Ray.

HIDDEN HURT REVEALED

As my conversation with the managers continued, Ray made his way to the office and picked up the phone. From the look on his face, it was immediately obvious that this was one of those dreaded phone calls bringing bad news. Twisting his body so that no one could see his face, Ray began to speak in soft tones of sympathetic love. Despite the continued conversation (which I left to the managers, who acted as if nothing was wrong), I could hear the words Ray was saying.

"Please don't cry, dear. Please. I know it hurts. I want to be there, but I can't leave my job. They'll fire me. Please don't cry. I can't leave." Sometimes you can't say the magic words to make things better; this was one of those times.

Looking at the side of Ray's face, I could see tears rolling down his cheek. I could clearly hear his muffled sobs and sniffles as the conversation between his bosses casually continued . . . for twenty minutes, then thirty. I have never witnessed a man trying as hard to control emotional pain as Ray did that day. When he finally hung up the phone, wiped the tears from his face, and took his first steps toward the office door, I could tell that he was mentally and physically exhausted.

In that state of mind Ray didn't need what happened next. The two managers of the terminal allowed Ray Barnes to walk out their door and go back to work while they said nothing to him. Only a self-absorbed adult brat incapable of emotional concern would do such a thing, and the coldhearted act caused me to instantly remember the most emotionally bereft delinquent I've ever known: my mastermind nemesis camper, John Morton.

Do you remember the episode when John led his buddies in a midnight escapade to find cigarettes? The blatant disregard for honesty and loyalty in that caper made John a poster boy for self-destructive behaviors. Yet John's struggle with lying and disloyalty wasn't even close to being his major challenge at the time. That would be his indifference to others.

"Indifferent" is a polite way of saying someone is unsympathetic, insensitive, and unfeeling. More to the point, John was coldheartedly compassionless. As his personality profile stated, "Pretrip testing reveals one serious flaw in John's character, that is, his indifference to other people. If this indifference could be changed to compassion for others, then he might recognize the negative effects of his delinquent actions."

I saw John do a lot of stupid things on that first camping trip (regrettably, he was still doing them on another trip with me a year later). But one of the things I never saw him do was express remorse to his campmates for his antics. Never an apology, never an acknowledgment of sensitivity to others. He was callous, just like Ray's supervisors.

Excusing myself from my conversation with the grain storage managers, I exited the office and caught up with Ray as he wandered back to the unloading area. Pulling him aside in an unoccupied office, I asked him the simple three-word question that his managers should have asked: "Ray, what's wrong?" Immediately he began sobbing uncontrollably and telling me of the trauma that was consuming his heart and soul. His wife had called him in near hysteria because their twenty-one-year-old son had just attempted suicide. After the young man was transported to a psychiatric hospital, where he was placed on suicide watch, the doctors would not allow her to see him.

Ray's wife needed him, but so did his company. So Ray was caught in a quandary: risk losing his job to go and comfort his wife or stay on the job while sacrificing his role as a husband. And what about his own hurting soul? Who would minister to that need? Not his company. They were content to let him walk back to a highly dangerous job when 100 percent of his emotional being was focused elsewhere.

My thought after talking with Ray was *If the company leaders are willing to do this and risk injuring Ray, could the same uncaring attitude have contributed to the injuries I am here to investigate?* Further investigation revealed that it had. The compassionless behavior of Ray's supervisors directly contributed to the three lost-time accidents. As Ray Barnes will tell you, it also contributed to an emotional scar that remains with him to this day.

Removing a Stake in the Heart

Of the three vital business values stolen by adult brats—honesty, loyalty, and compassion—it is the absence of compassion that inflicts the most damage on the moral fiber of the organization and the morale of the employee:

- George Ritter grieved more deeply over the death of his company's compassion for its employees than he did its new employment policies encouraging disloyalty.
- Anne Whiteman's decision to reveal the truth about her FAA coworkers was gut-wrenching, but the angst of whistle-blowing paled compared with the suffering she felt when her coworkers turned their back on her.
- Ray Barnes didn't mind sacrificing for his company, working copious amounts of overtime to satisfy the customer, but his managers' blatant neglect in recognizing his deeper commitment to his family wounded him severely, eventually causing him to look elsewhere for employment.

Ultimately, a business's failure to cultivate a culture of compassion can kill it, particularly as businesses increasingly depend on employee cooperation to weather difficult economic times.

If you are to rid your workplace of the callous behavior that destroys compassion, you will need a solution that not only demands a behavioral change from your adult brats but also a change of heart. That's the difference between climbing the first two mountains to retrieve honesty and loyalty and climbing the one you're on now to reclaim compassion.

Your first two conquests were achieved using trail rules that involved a battle of behavioral will. *Stay* within sight and sound: be transparent so the truth is known. *Come* to all huddle-ups: be accountable so that loyalty results. These are pure commands aimed at behavioral compliance. Don't get me wrong: succeeding at these is important, and they are difficult to get adult brats to achieve, as you have witnessed. But in this, the last stage of your mountaineering experience, your task is to energize the compassionless human heart of adult brats—or expose and eliminate them from influencing your work area. This is a duty more complex and daunting than anything you have yet learned because it involves answering a volatile question that cuts to the quick of moral fiber: *What stands in the way of the human heart committing itself to compassion?* (More to the point, it's like asking, what stood in the way of Ray's bosses offering him compassion? Later on I'll tell you.)

When you answer this question in practical terms, specific to your workplace, it points to obstacles you need to remove to create a compassionate work culture or, more pointedly, to identify and correct those who are without compassion.

When it came to my delinquents, the identification of such obstacles was easy, considering the nature of the most corrupting influences at the time. The trail rule we created to eliminate the obstructions was equally as simple, providing us a head start on building a culture of compassion in our camp groups.

RULE 3: CORRUPTION

The corruption rule: *You may not bring illegal drugs, alcohol, and tobacco products with you on your camping trip.*

Sounds a little legalistic for a rule aimed at conquering hearts, doesn't it? Then again, you likely haven't separated two kids in a mountain meadow about to kill each other over a contraband cigarette. Or tried to roust a drugged camper from his sleeping bag so that his hungry camp group can march down the trail to its food resupply point.

But I bet you have witnessed two workers who will say or do anything—honest or not—to win a promotion. Or you know a totally results-oriented manager who drives his employees beyond their breaking point to make himself look good. Perhaps you've even witnessed coworkers turn their backs on someone like Ray, who has a need for compassion.

If you're good-hearted, such lack of pity has most likely prompted you to ask the question I posed earlier. *What stands in the way of the human heart committing itself to compassion?* Perhaps you've already surveyed your workplace for obstacles to compassion. I'm curious. What did you find?

I've found one large obstacle that stands between the intent to exercise compassion and actually doing it. It's called *corruption*. The ancient Greeks had a word for it: *skolios*, meaning "crooked" or "curved." Today we use a derivative, *scoliosis*, as a medical term describing an abnormal lateral curvature of the spine.

Without being insensitive to those who suffer from this debilitating medical condition, I want to stress that *corrupt*, in its ancient sense, is an appropriate descriptor of those whose weakened backbone of character causes them to deviate (curve away) from responsible behavior when facing even the smallest of obstacles. *Corrupt* is also an accurate definition of the obstacle standing in the way of compassion, for such an obstruction causes people to curve away from the path of doing what is right.

In this sense, *corrupt* is an apt descriptor of both Ray's managers and the obstacles that prevented them from helping him. The managers' share of corruption is called the *personal corruption of compassion*. Like the personal factors of loss causation, this corruption is attributable mainly to the character the worker forms outside the influence of his work environment.

The primary obstacles to exercising workplace compassion typically come from organizational influences, namely the business environment, and thus we call this portion the *organizational corruption of compassion.* To be fair, a good amount of the organizational corruption of compassion is benign, consisting of obstacles created by the necessary evil of organizational structure and policies.

An example of a benignly created obstacle is the Health Insurance Portability and Accountability Act (HIPAA); this is the medical information law designed in part to prevent unauthorized access to medical records. At first glance, HIPAA seems like a smart law. But what if you have a coworker who suffers an injury or illness, you rush him to a medical facility, and later you call the medical facility on behalf of concerned colleagues who simply want to know how to best support their friend? You're out of luck; the facility can't tell you anything.

Most organizational corruption is not benign; it's willful, established in the organization by the collective effort of corrupt individuals who taint the good intentions of their company through either neglect or purpose. A little later, I'll share with you several examples of organizational obstacles created by this collective effort.

For now, we need to further examine the personal and organizational corruption of compassion to learn what obstacles need to be removed for compassion to begin. With my campers, it was the simple elimination of alcohol, drugs, and tobacco products. With Ray's managers, it was something far deeper.

PERSONAL CORRUPTION: EYES WIDE SHUT TO COMPASSION

Could it be that Ray's managers simply did not recognize that he had a personal need? As naive as this sounds, much of the personal corruption of compassion starts here. Many people are basically blind to human need. Compassion demands opening one's emotional eyes. Regrettably, the only one who had his eyes open during Ray's crisis was me.

The willing awareness of need was modeled for us by a historical figure who, in my mind, embodies the value of compassion more than any other: Abraham Lincoln, a man reviled by his critics for refusing to join the bloodlust of revenge at the end of the Civil War. Commenting on the extent of Lincoln's compassion, Carl Schurz said, "It is certainly true that he could not witness any individual distress or oppression, or any kind of suffering, without feeling a pang of pain himself, and that by relieving as much as he could the suffering of others he put an end to his own. This compassionate impulse to help he felt not only for human beings, but for every living creature."[1]

Notice the operative word here: "witness." Lincoln constantly had his eyes open to witness the need for compassion. He looked for it because he personally identified with the need for it. And there's the rub. The adult brat simply doesn't see the need for compassion.

A need is defined by the standards and values of the observer. What appears to be a need to one observer may not necessarily qualify as a need in the eyes of another. In Ray's case, both managers overheard his conversation and witnessed his agony. But since neither responded, we may conclude that they did not possess a sufficient standard to consider that anything was wrong with Ray. In this case, they were their own corrupting obstacle to compassion.

ORGANIZATIONAL CORRUPTION:
NO LOOK, NO LISTEN, NO FEEL

As guilty as they were individually, Ray's managers were also the victims of obstacles placed in their way by their company. Had they wanted to reach out to Ray, they would have encountered difficulties because of organizational limitations.

It's not that their company wanted them to be callous, at least not from outward appearances. Quite the opposite. I was present at a meeting where they were taught their company's mission statement. It said that the company was dedicated to maintaining "a balanced work environment between work commitments and duties, and family and community obligations."

When employees know better but fail to act on their knowledge, I smell a rat called *organizational corruption*. Ray's managers knew that their company would not hold them accountable for failing to show compassion, even though their company's mission statement indicated that they were to do otherwise. Additionally, they had never seen their company practice compassion with any of its employees. It didn't take them long to add up the formula provided them: no transparency of compassion plus no accountability for compassion equals no need to create compassion. If they ignored Ray, so what?

Reality may have been on the side of Ray's managers, but moral correctness was not. Researchers at the University of Michigan Business School define organizational compassion as the process in which organizational members collectively notice, feel, and respond to pain within their organization. Organizational compassion is evident in organizational behaviors.[2] If it were truly a compassionate organization, Ray's company would have assisted its employees in the practice of proactively looking, listening, and feeling for compassionate needs. Instead, it provided its employees with a well-meaning mission statement that had no backbone—a corrupt obstacle to overcome. It mirrors several other widely used adult bratlike business practices that inexplicably place obstructions in the way of employees who wish to care for others. Among these practices are the following. Do you recognize any from your place of employment?

- Businesses assign workers compassion-related job duties but don't teach them how to functionally express compassion.
- Businesses place workers in jobs where they are promised organizational compassion but are denied it when they need it.

- Businesses often "train out" of workers the compassionate attitude they bring to the job.
- Businesses uncompassionately force workers to make unnecessary priority choices between job and home.
- Businesses uncompassionately blame the worker first if anything goes wrong.

HIDING BEHIND PSEUDOCOMPASSION

Skirting responsibility for compassion in the workplace is easier now because the definition of compassion has become diluted. This dilution contributed to both the personal and the organizational corrupting of Ray's bosses.

Author George Will provides an excellent starting point for understanding a new diluted definition of compassion when he talks about "the emotive language of today's therapeutic ethos" substituting for the exercise of true compassion. Will builds a picture of an adult bratlike society in which using emotional language and expressing feelings of care are considered more important than providing tangible actions to alleviate personal pain. Thus it is considered sufficient for a politician to say "I feel good about this" or "I'm sorry about that" rather than to do something about it.[3]

Will was talking about politics, and yet this is also how adult brats devalue compassion in the workplace. They substitute empathy that makes them feel good for acts of compassion designed to make others feel good. It's pseudocompassion and not the real thing.

This type of false compassion was the hallmark of John Morton, mastermind juvenile delinquent. He could make his fellow campers feel as if he cared for their plight without doing anything about it. More than once I witnessed him lay forth his emotive baloney, assuage the angst of his campmates, and walk away with a smirk of successful manipulation.

What John knew is that empathy carries no determined response—he could have empathy without a commitment to do anything about it. The same thing happens in our workplaces every day. Imagine a group of employees meeting in the snack room and talking about the recent death of an absent employee's parent.

Employee A: Poor George, I really feel for him. I mean, how long was his father ill with cancer? Long time, wasn't it?

Employee B: Yeah, and he had to keep making those long trips out of town to his parents' house. Did you notice how tired he looked every Monday morning?

Employee C: Oh, so that was it. I just thought it was male menopause. You know how guys look when middle age starts setting in hard.

Employee A: We really ought to get him a card or something. I'll pitch in a few bucks if you will.

Employee C: Me, too.

Employee B: Okay, sounds good to me. I've got to run—big conference call in a few minutes. Catch you guys later.

You know the story's ending all too well. The consensus spurred by the emotive will of the group gets lost in the practical outworking of who is to buy the sympathy card, get it signed by the group, and give it to George. In the end, no one does. Feelings are considered to be enough. When George comes back to work, each employee can honestly say to him, "I was thinking about you during your time of need" or (in Clintonesque terms) "I feel your pain." How nice and therapeutic—and compassionately bankrupt.

Compassion demands more than empathy. This was the conclusion of researchers from the University of Michigan, who wrote, "We argue, however, that compassion differs from empathy in that compassion also involves being moved to respond to a person's suffering."[4] In other words, compassion must include action.

Discovering Real Compassion

Action was what Beckie Sweatman needed the most. Sweatman was a Dallas Independent School District (DISD) swimming coach whose battle with non-Hodgkin's lymphoma at age twenty-four spurred an outpouring of active compassion from her colleagues. Because she had less than two years' experience in the school district, Beckie did not qualify for extended sick leave. This concerned fellow coach Mike Zoffuto, who asked other DISD coaches if they would transfer some of their available sick leave days to Beckie's account.

And how Beckie's colleagues responded! As Coach Zoffuto told the *Dallas Morning News*, "I thought people might give her a day. Then I started counting, and they'd put down five, seven, four . . . and that's how she got all those days."[5] When Beckie Sweatman died at age twenty-six, with her Iraq War veteran husband at her side, the coaches of DISD had given her more than four hundred days of sick leave.

Empathy was not enough for those coaches, even when responding to the need of someone most of them barely knew.

You won't find this kind of proactive, must-respond definition of compassion in your standard dictionary. There, it is defined only as empathy or as "sympathetic pity and concern for the sufferings or misfortunes of others," from the Latin *compati*, to "suffer with."[6] You will, however, find compassion defined in its proactive sense in the writings and philosophy of the ancient Greeks and those influenced by their culture.

The classical Greek word for compassion is a variation of *splagna*, meaning "bowels." Now, don't get grossed out at this point. Hang with me. There's some important wisdom here about values in the workplace.

Compassion, in its original sense, is associated with the intestines—what we might call a gut feeling. One author says that ancient writers "may also have had in mind a physical feeling associated with compassion. Sometimes a sharp pain in the abdomen will accompany intense feelings of compassion or pity for those we love."[7] You know that feeling. It's the uneasy, sick-at-your-stomach feeling that makes you turn the television channel away from scenes of starving children in Third World countries. It's also what prompts you to make a donation to their relief, if you allow yourself to watch long enough.

Another writer puts it more bluntly. "The verb [compassion] means to 'move the bowels.' And it came to mean 'to move with compassion.' You might say that to not have compassion equals spiritual constipation."[8]

Constipation? Sounds like an appropriate description of the compassionless nonresponse to Ray Barnes by his supervisors. Sadly, it also describes Beto's camp group's frozen response to poor Jimmy Williams as he desperately clung to a rock face, paralyzed by fear. But unlike Ray's unhappy ending, a most unexpected source ultimately provided Jimmy with the compassion he needed. The story of how this happened is worth examining because it demonstrates how to break down the uncaring wall of adult brats in your workplace, placing you one significant step closer to eliminating their corrupting influence.

FREE TO CARE

When I say "poor Jimmy Williams," I mean what Southerners call "dirt poor." Fifteen-year-old Jimmy was on Beto and Bridgette's trip because he was labeled "at risk," meaning he hadn't been caught doing anything illegal but authorities felt he was likely to commit an offense.

Truth is, Jimmy's thin body and shaved head, scarred by head lice, gave less sensitive people the creeps. He looked like an indigent, straight out of a Depression-era soup line. Such tragedy happens when your next meal isn't guaranteed, you have no permanent place to sleep, your mother is in a mental institution, and your closest male relatives have all committed suicide. That was Jimmy.

He was alone and many times he fended for himself. If there ever was a poster boy for needing compassion, Jimmy was it, and he got it from his campmates, at least for a short time.

Perhaps his new friends gave him a small part of their heart because opposites attract and Jimmy was their polar opposite. They were emotionally weak but physically strong; Jimmy was puppy-dog friendly but a ninety-eight-pound weakling. They bore the tag of juvenile delinquents; as yet, he hadn't acquired the label. Whatever the reason, he had not only instantly been accepted by everyone in the group, but in fact they proactively sought to help him. Even little Victor, himself the product of a horrific family background, offered to carry some of Jimmy's camp gear.

The emotional reservoir of troubled kids is at best limited, and as the trip progressed, Jimmy's helplessness wore on his buddies. By the time we rappelled into the secluded mountain valley blessed by Bridgette's screams, they had turned on him. Help became harping, which produced in Jimmy the opposite effect than it would have in insensitive delinquents. They stonewalled, effortlessly deflecting criticism; he cried, easily falling to pieces in a demonstrative helplessness that at once left you both heartbroken and annoyed.

It was amazing, then, that Jimmy completed his rappel into the valley without trauma. He leaned out into space and zipped down the rappel line without hesitating.

You can be brave when not knowing what you're facing. That had been the salvation of Jimmy's life. He was an innocent, rolling with the punches as life propelled him backward, like a rappel, into horrendous situations he could not see coming. Jimmy had grown accustomed to living life in a backing-up mode. As long as he could not see the problems coming, he could cope.

Unfortunately for Jimmy, there is no way to perform a rock climb backward. It is an obstacle that must be faced head-on, with eyes open. As I set up the rock climbing route that would lead us out of the valley, what little hold Jimmy had on his emotional composure began to fade. He began to weep quietly, realizing that the route we took into the valley was the one that led out. If he hoped to go back to civilization, he must stare his challenge in the face and conquer it one handhold at a time.

There was no such sweat for me; I basically had the day off. After climbing up the rock face and securing the climbing rope at the top, I turned over rock-climbing instructor duties to another staff member. Not finding a Starbucks nearby, I decided to rappel halfway down the cliff to a rock ledge where I could take pictures of the kids and offer verbal encouragement during their climb.

Several climbers took their turn before Jimmy did, and none of them experienced much difficulty. It wasn't a hard climb, technically, unless you were a rookie. In that case, the seventy-five-foot ascent resembled Mount Everest. For Jimmy, as he began his climb, it probably looked more like outer space.

Climbing tenuously past the ten-foot mark, Jimmy treated each foot grip and handhold as if it were untrustworthy. By the arduous labor it took him to make simple moves, I could tell Jimmy's climb was going to end in a stall. Sure enough, exhausted by muscle fatigue and the energy expended by crying, Jimmy froze at the twenty-foot level, paralyzed by a fear born of insecurity. No words of encouragement I shouted seemed to help. Defeatism had won, urged on by the words of derision thrown at him by his once-compassionate teammates.

Taking command, I yelled instructions to lower Jimmy to the ground using his safety (belay) rope. Once down, he ran to a nearby rock and began to sob uncontrollably, crushed. Even thirty feet off the ground, I could hear his cries.

Angrily, I shouted at the handful of campers whose barbs had contributed to Jimmy's failure, "Why don't you do something to help him?"

My bad. I didn't define "something," leaving it to irresponsible campers to devise their own plan of action. As a spectator, I watched the plan unfold.

Grabbing Jimmy forcefully by his arms, three of the larger boys, Beto included, literally dragged him to the other side of a large boulder, out of sight and sound of the climbing instructor. There they were joined by the remaining campers.

I was tempted to call a huddle-up because of the sight-and-sound rule, but, like the rappel, the group was too spread out to effectively use one. Besides, from my vantage point, I could technically see what was going on; I just couldn't hear it. All I could do was sit back and trust that whatever was being done by the kids was compassionate, not harmful.

Compassionate? Judging by the energetic arm flailing and finger pointing at Jimmy, the group was anything but compassionate. I've seen prison guards act more kindly. But between moments of animation and obvious confronting behavior, the group calmed down and appeared to be listening to Jimmy. Maybe something good was happening after all.

Reappearing from their hiding place, Beto asked the instructor if Jimmy could be the next climber. Yes, he could. Sensing there was a mood change in the group, Jimmy was quickly hooked in and sent on his way up.

If the team's input had made any difference, it didn't show at first. Jimmy plodded along at the same speed as before, and I could again see him crying. But this time, as he drew closer to me, I began to pick up the sound of muttering mixed with sniffles and sobs. A few feet higher, and I could distinguish a few words of the utterance.

"I can do all things," he would say and then his voice would trail off into a whimper. "I can do all things," I heard again more clearly.

Then it hit me. What had happened behind the rock was more than compassion; it was a miracle. Out of love and concern, the group had taught Jimmy a short Bible verse to encourage him to complete his climb. As he slowly ascended past me, he kept repeating the scripture in rhythm with his sobs. "I can do all things . . . sob, sniffle . . . I can do all things . . . sob." Reaching the top, without yielding to the fear that had previously stopped him, he knew he could.

Stirring a Compassion That Beats Adult Brats

Jimmy was not the only one to benefit from my abrasive challenge for his group to act compassionately; the entire group profited. Their sustained cheers rang through the valley as Jimmy reached the top of his climb, evidence of a values-based unity of purpose that did not exist beforehand.

Translating what happened on the rock that day into actionable steps to overcome personal and organizational obstacles to compassion is not an exact science. But from it, we can take away several guidelines that will place you on a path to building a caring culture that counters the corrupting influence of adult brats, potentially changing them as it did my camp group. Just imagine if Ray's company and its bosses had tried any of the following four guidelines.

1. Always Assume That Problems Demanding Compassion Will Exist

I could have turned my back on Jimmy, convincing myself that he had no special need. You know these arguments of conscience because at one point or another you've thought them. *Everyone has problems; what makes him different? He doesn't have a need; he's just a crybaby. A little reality will do him good, toughen him up.*

In the business world, obstacles to compassion start when we convince ourselves that no one has a need. This jaded attitude grows out of organizational obstacles to compassion. We are encouraged to think we can tolerate lying and disloyalty because they are accepted parts of corporate life. After all, you need to grease the skids of your career path by lying a little bit every now and then. Disloyalty? It's unavoidable as you job-hop your way up the corporate ladder. So why can't you be just as ignorant about compassion in the workplace? After all, who needs to act compassionately in the business world?

Those who rationalize like this end up wounding others, as Ray's bosses did.

2. Put the Job Description Away and Put on an Air of Caring

Compassion doesn't care about rank. I was the big boss of the camp group. Big deal. Jimmy had a need; asking the group to do something to help Jimmy was a no-brainer. I would have done it regardless of my position within the group.

An employee's rank, authority, or job description often gets in the way of caring for coworkers. Those of higher rank may fear looking "soft" and losing the effectiveness of their command; lower-ranking employees may feel a lack of empowerment to help. These are organizational obstacles of the worst kind, blockages of personal worth created by the business organization.

I know the former executive vice president of the world's largest company within its industry sector. When his company purchased a much smaller company, my friend spent several weeks visiting each of the purchased company's business units, telling the employees how much he cared for them, asking them to stay with their new organization. He could have sent an HR representative or midlevel manager to greet the new employees, but he didn't. He genuinely cared for those employees and recognized the insecurity they felt at the time.

3. Allow the Team to Work in a Compassionate Mode without Preset Limits or Methods

Giving my troubled kids free rein to devise a support effort for Jimmy was a gamble based on a modicum of accumulated trust. Our group had moved past the acceptable hanging or flogging stage, so I felt I could anticipate a reasonably acceptable plan of action, if one developed.

Still, I was surprised that the group's plan involved scripture memorization. Though it was an unconventional approach, it was obviously a strategy with which the group felt comfortable. That was good enough for me.

Preconceived ideas of how and when compassion should be exercised in the workplace stand little chance of acceptance by independent-minded adult brats. If you are going to use compassion at work as a force to entice adult brats to maturity, it's best to give them the freedom to choose how to do it.

4. Approach Compassion as a Personal Outreach, Not a Corporate Directive

As mentioned, the wilderness therapy credo is "Prepare by instruction; learn by experience." Jimmy had been instructed; his climb was the experience. I could have kicked back and let Jimmy cry himself into a state of irretrievable self-pity. I'd done my job.

But because I had interviewed those who knew his history of neglect and his family's struggle with mental illness, I was aware when Jimmy needed an extra measure of compassion. My heart was compelled to intercede on his behalf, credo or not.

There is no substitute for getting to know those who work around you and to value them personally. If you don't know them as individuals—know the names of their spouses and kids, where they live, where they're from—then you will be unable to recognize their need for compassion when it happens. A good first step is simply to ask them about themselves, then listen to them. Put on your compassionate ears before they need your compassionate action. Don't get caught trying to fake your understanding of someone else's real need. That's a hole from which you can't climb out.

HOMEWARD BOUND

Reaching the peak of Mount Compassion is both exasperating and rewarding. Gratification comes from recovering the value of compassion from adult brats, even learning how to use it to meet their deep needs and bring them into maturity. Anxiety results when you realize the immense challenge that awaits you in the real world of business, where you must apply everything you've learned.

I empathize. I knew how to help people discover the principles of honesty, loyalty, and compassion when Art Rollins called me to help him with his employees, but that didn't stop me from shaking in my boots at the thought of doing it in his business.

Despite these emotions at this point in our journey, a more powerful feeling will overcome you as you sit on the summit. It's happiness. You're headed home. You've traversed the mountain range, surviving rock climb and rappel, and now, from the top of Mount Compassion, you see nothing but descent before you. In the distance, you think you see a town.

Like clockwork, your mind switches gears away from the wilderness and back to civilization—real food, a bed, warmth, and a shower. Go ahead, feel happy. You deserve it.

But if you think this is the end, you're wrong. Your journey has one last twist, an added lesson in values without which everything you learned thus far is rendered void. So before you get fixated on stuffing your face with pizza, you had better put your feet back on the ground and pay attention to where you're going and the reason you're on this trip with me.

Chapter Nine

Winning the Jerk Revolution

Jack Butler was not a man to mince words. As a member of the "greatest generation," Jack saw things in black and white, not shades of gray, and he didn't have much patience for putting forth an effort without getting a result. In that regard, he was much like my father, which is why his no-nonsense question didn't surprise me.

"When am I going to see some results?" he asked gruffly.

It wasn't as if I could wave my magic wand. I'd been consulting with his large manufacturing company for only two months. But it was long enough to have glimpsed the systemic character problems plaguing Jack's manufacturing plant. Those problems became clear the moment I held a meeting with his floor supervisors and suggested they might do more to bridge the teamwork gap between their rank and the floor workers.

"That's ludicrous," blurted out a supervisor named Chuck Philbrick. "It's their duty to come to me, not for me to go to them. I'm the boss."

Pausing to allow the arrogant aroma of his comment to dissipate, I decided that Chuck's response deserved an appropriate reply. So I asked him, "What's the most important piece of equipment on your manufacturing floor?"

You could see the wheels turning in his mind as Chuck struggled to think of a safe answer to prevent him from falling into the diabolical trap he suspected I was laying for him. Sweat trickled from his brow. His feet tapped nervously. Finally, having settled on what he thought was the safest answer he could give, he said, "The fire extinguisher."

"Okay," I calmly replied. Then I asked the supervisor sitting next to him the same question. After a similar period of nervous contemplation, the supervisor replied, "The fire extinguisher."

Progressing to the next supervisor, she screamed, "Fire extinguisher!" before I could even complete my question to her. On around the circle of twenty supervisors gathered in the room the mantra persisted, each one rapidly answering "Fire extinguisher," until I reached the next-to-last supervisor in the gathering.

His reply? "The human brain."

Like a temblor causing a bunch of bobblehead dolls to shake in unison, all the supervisors nodded their heads in affirmation, pointing their fingers at the purveyor of truth in declaration of his wisdom. So intense was the shaking of heads, I felt a momentary twinge of motion sickness.

"Yep, that's exactly what I was thinking," said one supervisor in a rear-end saving move.

"People are important," shouted another.

Similar verbal confirmations followed, leaving me to ask the group the mother of all rhetorical questions. "If that's what you really think, why didn't you say so in the first place?"

The answer, as you surmise, sat there glaring at me. It was Chuck Philbrick and the deeply engrained influence he (and a group of his peers) held over the attitude of others. If he thought a fire extinguisher was most important, so did everyone else. And if he considered it beneath himself to build teamwork with his subordinates, that might explain a good deal of Jack Butler's problems.

Breaking this stranglehold of adult brat brotherhood would not be easy or fast. Jack would need to exercise patience—a character trait he did not possess.

Two months into the battle (barely the equivalent of a few miles down the trail on the journey to ridding Jack's business of its adult brat influence), he demanded a miracle for his money. Like many parents who brought their "broken" children to me, wanting me to fix complex personal problems with a relatively short wilderness expedition, Jack harbored an unrealistic expectation of the effort it takes to successfully battle the hideous strength that confines people to immaturity. He also failed to recognize the role his personal resolve played in the battle.

Attempting to bring reality to Jack's expectations, I again explained the long-term process of restoring the values Chuck and his buddies had stolen from the company. Apart from totally removing the adult brats from his supervisory staff—a move not economically feasible—Jack needed to wage the persevering battle of heart and will I've described in previous chapters.

Trying again to get me to give him the quick-fix answer he wanted, Jack asked, "Well, then, how are we going to win this battle?"

I knew he was expecting me to announce some grandiose plan that would, in one sweeping motion, cure all his employee problems. But I instead told Jack the truth. "One employee at a time," I said.

My answer didn't please Jack. He didn't want to wage a heart battle, much less a battle of will with his supervisors. Jack was old school, a man who thought money paid to employees—and he paid his employees well—should buy the right to demand that they change their attitude.

Shortly after our talk, Jack gave up. He terminated my services, leaving Jack's adult brat supervisors to ply their self-serving, economically crippling havoc among line-level employees. Eventually Jack sold his company, bringing him retirement money. But he never knew the deep satisfaction that Art Rollins, Suzanne Miller, and others have experienced from waging the battle until victory results.

IMPATIENCE: A SELF-INFLICTED WOUND

Adult brats are to blame for the theft of several values vital to business success, but patience isn't one of them; its disappearance is a self-inflicted offense. As Jack Butler demonstrates, the number-one enemy in the struggle against adult brats is sometimes you, the responsible employee or employer who recognizes the problem, attempts to do something about it, but loses patience in the process.

Perhaps the culprit is someone who works in your office, like Jennifer Cohen. Remember Cohen's story from chapter 4? She is the twenty-something "employee gone wild" who continued to abuse her company's policy on casual dress despite being confronted by an older colleague.

Let's say you're that older female colleague. Cohen has initially rejected your attempts to counsel her, and now you've decided to use the combined personal powers of transparency, accountability, and compassion to change her for the better. Part of your strategy is to dress according to company policy, to enlist several others in the office to casually give you compliments about your outfits within earshot of Cohen, and to reward Cohen's acceptable dress choices through positive verbal reinforcement. You even invite her to a trendy lunch spot with other coworkers in an attempt to bridge the generation gap.

Although you begin to see gradual improvement in Cohen's dress, there are days when she reverts to ignoring the company's dress code, complaining that the code is unfair to her generation and that it violates her freedom of expression.

On one such day, when Cohen mounts her generational soapbox, you lose all patience and snap at her, telling her to "grow up." Bitter words follow, bringing to futility the exercise of all your value-based personal powers. She exits the confrontation more determined than ever to remain an adult brat, convinced you are no better than she is.

Have you ever experienced something similar? Go ahead and raise your hand if you've been guilty; I'll wait. If you haven't, I'll bet you know a well-meaning coworker who has.

I've confessed many of my temptations to short-circuit the very process I advocate to you in these pages. Those who know me best will never say that patience is one of my strengths. But for sheer impatience, albeit in face of the toughest times, I nominate

Mitch Grant, my trip counselor who twice had to endure wilderness excursions with the mistress of patience testers, Shawna Washington. For those of us who suffer from impatience in the battle with adult bratlike immaturity, their story demonstrates how we gather strength to endure to its end.

THE DILEMMA OF PATIENCE

At the time of Mitch's employment, daily activities during each trip were documented by way of an audiocassette recording (yes, I know this dates me), serving as a trip log. Trip counselors would gather together after the campers were put to bed, rehash the events of the day, make significant observations about each camper, then record their findings.

After the trip, the audiotapes were transcribed to a written format, providing the most accurate indicator of the stress level of counselors. On the tapes (considered by staff to be a safe haven for emotional release), the raw emotions of counselors often accompanied a report of the salient details of the day. Listening to a tape revealed the extraordinary lengths to which counselors patiently sacrificed their true feelings about campers to offer them help.

On the Richter scale of emotional force, no counselor communicated the stress of this sacrifice more poignantly than Mitch, one of my most effective and yet patience-challenged staff members. Although years younger than Jack Butler, Mitch shared Jack's results-oriented, take-no-prisoners impatience with behavioral disorder, and there was no prisoner Mitch wanted to take more badly than the one who tested his patience the most: Shawna Washington.

No one could make Mitch's blood pressure rise faster than Shawna. Sent to us by adoptive parents who wanted us to "fix" her emotional bonding problems, Shawna could play the victim's role better than any disadvantaged youth I've known. Her pity parties had not set well with Mitch when she participated on a fourteen-day trip with him the previous year, and I was afraid that she would push all of Mitch's buttons during her second trip with him, a more physically challenging twenty-one-day expedition. Mitch and two other counselors conducted the trip while I remained at camp headquarters.

Despite some rough moments early in their trip, when Shawna's initial whining rankled Mitch, the two managed to peacefully endure the gradual uphill journey to the true test of the trip— the high mountains of Colorado's Sangre de Cristo Wilderness Preservation Area. Mitch, sounding on tape less stressed than I had anticipated, even managed to record some positive comments about Shawna in his trip audio log:

> Shawna has been unflappable. A good hiker who carries more than her fair share of the load. Shawna has done everything physically that she has been asked to do. It is almost as if she needs a greater physical challenge to unmask her base emotions. They still have not surfaced.

This was the cooperative Shawna I had hoped would show up for the trip; too bad she wasn't the one who stayed on the trip. Soon after Mitch's encouraging log entry, difficulties with Shawna began. As he predicted, the stress of high-altitude mountaineering surfaced Shawna's base emotions, and they were ugly. Selfishness, self-pity, and a loathing for others poured forth, resulting in many huddle-ups. In disgust, her peers quit offering her compassion and incentive to change. What good is it to offer help that's clearly not wanted?

But to everyone's surprise, as the group encountered the physical hardship of ascending well above the timberline, Shawna hung in there despite testing the resolve of the group with her attention-seeking passive-aggressive antics. When the group reached the ultimate physical challenge of the trip, a same-day climb of two peaks each standing higher than 13,000 feet, she successfully, but slowly, climbed both.

This is where Shawna's story takes an unhappy turn. Her time atop the twin peaks should have been a celebratory experience, perhaps a life-changing point in her life. But as the adage states, Shawna was determined to snatch defeat from the jaws of victory. Listen to Mitch describe her literal downhill turning point in his trip log from that day. See if you can hear the extreme exasperation and an unfortunate sense of resignation in his voice when it comes to Shawna. "It [a request Mitch had made of Shawna] didn't faze her at all. She just kept on slowing down the group. It was as if she had a death wish."

Do you hear it? If you can't, perhaps this will help.

Mitch recorded this after his group had survived a lightning storm that threatened the group as they descended a ridge immediately below the twin peaks. At the time of the storm, the group was hiking at an altitude of 12,000 feet, exposed, vulnerable to both the vicious forces of nature and the manipulation of anyone who wanted to die. The latter, it seemed, was Shawna.

Choosing this time as the optimum moment to stage a prolonged fit of self-pity and possible self-destruction, Shawna virtually quit on the group, delaying its lifesaving descent down the ridge. (Remember the sight-and-sound rule? Everyone stays together.) Her slow pace and frequent stops resulted in a quick huddle-up where Mitch explained the obvious safety danger and made one request of her: Would she please move faster?

No, she wouldn't. Talk about a patience tester.

Later that night, I received an emergency radio call from Mitch, informing me that he felt Shawna should be terminated from the trip. His reasons, apart from the understandable onetime safety concern she had presented, were at best flimsy.

She's causing too many huddle-ups, he said.

She's a troubled youth, and this is a trip for such kids, I replied.

She won't listen to anything I say, he complained.

Maybe you haven't reached the point of breakthrough with her that you want, I retorted.

I can't take her any longer, he finally blurted out.

Patience, I counseled.

In the end, Mitch recorded in his log the decision we reached that night. "The decision was reached to allow Shawna to continue on the trip and face 'teachable moments,' and the group should be challenged to help her out as much as possible."

What Mitch didn't add to his log was "Ron talked me out of being impatient," because as we both knew, impatience was the real reason Mitch used valuable battery life on his emergency radio to call me that night. Mitch wanted a Jack Butler solution, and I wouldn't let him have it.

The Long and Not-So-Short of It

I hope you've gotten a sense of the dynamic dilemma of patience. It challenges you at the most unexpected times. Just when you think you've successfully endured the worst, a greater, unanticipated trial follows, testing your fortitude as never before.

This was Mitch's problem in dealing with Shawna. He was caught by surprise at where and when he needed to exercise the most patience with her. It wasn't during her slow, halting ascent to the high-altitude mountain peaks, as he figured it might be. It was on her downhill journey, seemingly the easiest part of the journey—unless you're trying to outrun lightning.

Then there's the matter of circumstance. Don't think for a moment that Shawna didn't understand the psychological advantage provided by the crucial need to get off the ridge quickly. By slowing down, she had the group just where she wanted them—captives to her behavioral whim. If she could use the moment to wring every last ounce of patience out of Mitch, so much the better. Watching him explode in anger, or panic because of safety concerns, was a victory for her, a signal that no one controlled her.

This is often how it is with the adult brats who challenge your patience at work. Just when you think you've survived the worst of their behavior, it appears again. They know how to pick the "lightning strike" of opportunities to fight back when you, your company, or their boss is most vulnerable. At such times, they want you to become impatient; in fact, their continued immaturity depends on you giving up.

To empower their resistance to change, they depend on you forgetting the original meaning of patience, as Mitch did. Writers of ancient Middle East wisdom literature used the word 'arek for patience. Literally, it means "to make long" or "to prolong." The idea is to go slow all the time, resisting any temptation to speed up, get angry, or become frustrated, thus easing any pain that might accrue as the end of the journey draws near.

These writers came from a society whose perspective was amazingly the same then as ours is today. They knew that the end of the journey is better than the beginning, and they knew what it was like to get somewhere on foot, carrying their provisions with them. To get to where you're going, they were saying, you need to exercise a patience of spirit. Or, as my father always exhorted me, "Hang in there."

In business terms, it means committing to the long, steady task of ridding your workplace of adult brats, then not abandoning it (something Jack Butler could never grasp). This is hard because it means developing a slower reaction time to the continued bad behavior of adult brats, not allowing them to provoke you to impatience as the journey to defeat them nears its end.

Let me put it bluntly: don't be a knee-jerk reactionary, sabotaging yourself just as you are on the cusp of victory. That's what Shawna wanted Mitch to do—give up and release her from the trip, ending any expectations that she might achieve her personal growth goals. Listen to what Mitch recorded in the trip log the day after Shawna endangered the group on their descent from 13,598-foot Electric Peak (yes, that's the actual name of the mountain where the lightning storm happened): "Today during a huddle-up, Shawna admitted to the fact that yesterday she wanted to slow down for the purpose of being kicked off the trip. She didn't want to run away; she wanted to have the staff make the decision for her to leave."

A day earlier, Mitch was about to give Shawna the equivalent of what Jack Butler gave his adult brats: freedom from pressure to change, an excuse to remain immature, and a license to wreak havoc on his business, all because he lost sight of the meaning of patience. Now, fortified instead by both my exhortation and Shawna's confession of intent, Mitch marshaled the group into creating pressure for Shawna to change during the last few days of the trip. It was not easy, as Mitch's trip log from the first day after Electric Peak indicates:

> During the course of about an hour and a half or two hours we had several huddle-ups on Shawna. Basically they all had the same theme to the fact that she needed to change her attitude. After about the fifth huddle-up, she started answering us in a little bit more intelligent sentences, maybe like six words. After about the sixth huddle-up, it took us an excruciating long time to convince Shawna, but finally she said it on her own, that she needed to change her attitude.

Think the victory was won then? Guess again. Here's Mitch's log from the following day: "Had a huddle-up on Shawna a couple of times just within thirty minutes before we got on the trail. Basically, it's the same story, the same scenario."

On and on it went for several more days until, finally, Mitch records good news:

> In a huddle-up, Shawna agreed to sign a contract saying, "I, Shawna W., will make a change for the better in my attitude and make it fun for myself and for my group members." That statement seemed to help a little bit. Shawna's group influenced her to say she was going to have a good time and that she was going to cooperate.

This time it worked, but not in any miraculous sense. No bells rang as when Clarence the angel earned his wings in *It's a Wonderful Life*. No lightning bolt struck; no trumpets sounded. Yet for the remainder of her trip, Shawna exhibited a willingness to change her behavior. Here's what Mitch said about her near the end of the trip: "Shawna has stopped testing the staff. She hiked strongly, encouraged other campers, using tactics previously used on her to get her going. She has clearly adopted a go-with-the-flow attitude and seems less stressed."

In the absence of a dramatic turning point, what can explain such a turnaround? I have one word: *patience*. Long and slow is always better than quick and done.

HOW TO AVOID IMPATIENCE

Perhaps you think I'm being too hard on Mitch. After all, if you were in his shoes, dodging lightning strikes because of Shawna's fits of temperament, you might have made an emergency call to me much earlier . . . to get *you* off the trip.

In fairness, during the years Mitch served as a counselor in my wilderness program, he showed me many wonderful attributes. But Mitch's battle with impatience represents a common weakness that unites us all. At one point or another, we grow impatient over fighting the personal immaturity we find in our workplace, exposing our own frailties in the process.

To strengthen you, I offer these insights from Mitch's struggle with Shawna. These four guidelines will help you avoid impatience during the long-term struggle with adult brats.

1. Avoid Entertaining Too Many Preconceived Ideas about the Personal Character of the Adult Brat You Battle

Your preconception about someone's character may not reflect reality, especially if you've taken the liberty to "fill in the blanks" of the person's life with your own biases. If you undertake to correct or confront someone based on an incomplete or inaccurate picture of this person's total being, you will quickly grow impatient when he or she doesn't respond to you. Even if you are correct in identifying someone's behavior as adult bratlike, you may not possess a complete grasp of the character issues driving that person to immaturity.

Exhibit A for this mistake is Mitch. Shawna had participated on a previous trip with Mitch a year earlier, but a year in an adolescent's life is like a decade in adult time. Mitch didn't stop to consider how Shawna might have changed in the interim. Nor did he inquire about any pressures currently shaping her life that didn't exist a year ago. He launched into the second year's trip with a first-year frame of reference, labeling her a troublemaker from the start and quickly becoming frustrated with Shawna when she matched the reality he had created for her.

The workplace is frequently like a middle school. Reputations are unjustifiably gained and lost in a heartbeat. I once encountered a midlevel manager who couldn't wait for me to visit his work area and "straighten out" one of his shift supervisors, a hapless guy named Eddie Dolan. According to the manager, Eddie was uncooperative and excessively defensive. No one could even ask Eddie how the work flow was progressing on his shift without Eddie circling the wagons and shooting first. Derisively and openly, his manager called him "Nervous Neddie."

As I quickly discovered in a private talk with Eddie, a disability prevented him from processing information the way his boss wanted. He hadn't informed his manager about his disability because he feared that his reputation would be further tainted.

It took only a few minutes for me to help Eddie develop a manageable way to report his work information. My talk with his manager about impatience lasted much longer.

2. Avoid Allowing Your Peer Group to Unduly Reinforce Your Bias against the Adult Brat

Developing a lynch mob mentality against adult brats in your workplace will always result in short-tempered, impatient actions. Even well-intentioned leaders who seek to positively influence the work environment by ridding it of adult brats can overstep the bounds of patience. By surrounding themselves with like-minded colleagues who pressure them to take extremes, such leaders can easily lose patience (as well as their popularity with coworkers) when adult brats do not respond as desired.

Mitch Grant was guilty of such an error, as my posttrip staff interviews confirmed. Mitch's strong personality quickly solicited the support of group members—counselors as well as kids—who shared his open frustration with Shawna. A mob attitude developed, and despite the positive role that peer pressure played in eventually forcing Shawna to mature, the mob contributed to Mitch's impatience with her. In essence, Mitch became part of the problem that exacerbated his impatience.

When I visited Eddie Dolan's work area at lunchtime, as described earlier, this type of mob mentality already existed. Eddie sat alone in the corner of the workshop, trapped like a rat, while his coworkers and manager, Mike Mitchell, glared at him from behind their lunch pails. I halfway expected to see a firing squad.

Mike was the picture of fire-breathing impatience, a temperament fed by his not-so-merry band of workers, people who expected Mike to "do something" about Eddie. It's just that Mike didn't know what to do. Every time Eddie rejected Mike's awkward attempts to help, the work group became more impatient, putting more pressure on Mike to get results. This, in turn, led to his becoming more impatient.

Lost in the escalating cycle of frustration was the solution: Eddie's confidence in the group to help him with his disability. He felt he couldn't be transparent with his coworkers, telling them the *truth* about his disability. In turn, his coworkers perceived he had a *loyalty* problem, because Eddie would not let them hold him accountable. With no loyalty factor evident and no truth transparent, no *compassion* was offered to Eddie. Instead, impatience reigned.

3. Avoid the Shortsighted Exhaustion of the Temporal by Looking Ahead for Teachable Moments

Impatience is a natural companion of exhaustion. If you've ever attempted to confront or change a character-challenged individual, you know the vast amount of emotional energy it takes to succeed and the exhaustion it brings. Adult brats have a way of dragging you into an energy-sapping struggle, preventing you (if you let them) from looking ahead to where the greatest chance of helping them may lie—the teachable moment.

If you allow jerks on the job to keep you slogging away with them in the frozen tundra of struggle, they've won. Your patience won't last, and they know it.

If, however, you exercise patience and foresight, not yielding to the temptation to fight adult brats where they want you to go, you can actually predict when a teachable moment will occur and prepare to help them at that point. Regrettably, Mitch didn't do this.

Mitch fell victim to thinking the uphill climb to Electric Peak was where the battle of wills with Shawna had to be won. That's because she sucked him into several minibattles there, and he accommodated her by putting all his emotional energy into those battles. Her tactic is similar to what Jennifer Cohen, our dress-code-breaking adult brat, used against her work supervisor. She kept gnawing away at the rules, dragging the boss into exhausting battles, and she knew that the boss's impatience would ultimately cause her to give up.

You can sense Mitch's similar thinking pattern, only from the good guy's perspective. If Shawna didn't improve during the arduous uphill climb, nothing could be done to help her. She might as well be kicked off the trip.

In his shortsighted strategy to allow Shawna to define the battleground, Mitch forgot an important point. For most people, consistent downhill hiking is more difficult than uphill. That's because our hips and knees absorb the constant force of the back-pack's weight during each downhill step, causing body fatigue and pain at a rate greater than found while climbing uphill. Could it be that Shawna's teachable moment, when fatigue would exhaust her resistance to authority, might come after ascending Electric Peak instead of before? Mitch never knew; he was too busy fighting a current battle.

Stop and think. Look ahead. Step out of the mire your adult brats have created for you. Plot where you stand the greatest chance of winning your battle with them, and then have the patience to wait until they step into the teachable moment.

4. Do Not Get Caught without Assistance to Offer When the Adult Brat Decides to Change for the Better

Another by-product of the long-term fight against adult brats is forgetfulness, as in, *What was I thinking when I set out to do battle with these characters?* Sometimes, after the ache has gone away, we remember. *That's right. I was out to save my workplace from being destroyed by overgrown juvenile delinquents.* Sadly, by that time, frustration from impatience has wiped away any noble concept of how we planned to accomplish the task. Even if an adult brat reaches the teachable moment, impatience has robbed us of any clue about how to help.

This is where Mitch didn't let anyone down. Toward the end of his trip with Shawna, after miles of battering downhill travel and numerous huddle-ups, she indicated that she wanted to change, agreeing to sign a written contract stating as much. But where did the contract come from? It wasn't part of my program's standard issue to counselors, ready to whip out at a teachable moment's notice. No, it came from the mind of Mitch Grant.

Racing from the huddle-up to grab a pencil and a sheet of paper from the counselor's medical log, Mitch quickly wrote the contract I mentioned earlier. "I, Shawna W., will . . ." After surviving more than two weeks on the trail with Shawna, during which he'd been chastised by me and had committed more mistakes than either of us wanted, Mitch wasn't going to be cheated out of victory. Mitch may have shared many of Jack Butler's traits, but he was no Jack Butler. When he saw an opportunity to finish the job, he took it.

For sheer tenacity in holding out hope to an adult brat employee who didn't want it, refusing to quit until the employee agreed to change, it has to be Art Rollins. One of Art's misfits was DeWayne Kidrick, a truck mechanic whose battle with alcohol was the subject of both rumor and humor among Art's trucking company employees.

Although Art never caught DeWayne drunk at work, Art had nonetheless witnessed DeWayne's indiscriminate taste for alcohol at company social events and other small-town community functions. Once, DeWayne's wife called Art late at night, informing him that DeWayne was out on the streets drunk, cruising in the family's only vehicle. Would Art help her find him before it was too late?

Heading out into the pouring rain, Art found DeWayne's vehicle stuck in the median of the town's only divided highway. DeWayne was still in the driver's seat, pushing the accelerator to its limit. As Art approached the vehicle, DeWayne rolled down his window and shouted, "You better step back, Arty. I'm going a hundred miles an hour."

The man needed help, but if his work performance didn't suffer, what was Art to do? Time and again, to no avail, Art would usher DeWayne into his office to ask if he was okay. The answer was always the same: "No problem. Everything's fine."

Several months later the lie caught up with DeWayne. An employee reported seeing him drink from a medicine bottle he had brought with him to work, but the chugging action didn't resemble that of anyone downing the unpleasant taste of medicine. DeWayne was busted. Drinking on the job warranted an automatic employment termination under Art's employee policies, but Art had been prepared for this moment for years. Up to that point, he had not allowed impatience to cause him to give up on DeWayne; it didn't then either.

Calling me into an intervention session with DeWayne the next day, Art allowed me to confront DeWayne about the extent of his problem. After offering several excuses, just as Shawna did when she slowed down her group, DeWayne finally admitted his problem and agreed to seek help. From my carrying case, I quickly grabbed a piece of blank paper. On it I wrote, "I, DeWayne K., will . . ."

YOU ARE HERE ON THE MAP

For years I've kept a favorite cartoon near my desk. It shows a confused adult camper looking at a map while standing in the middle of a forest. The puzzled look on the camper's face portrays his dilemma: he's lost. On the map, his source of orientation, is an arrow accompanied by large letters saying, "You were here, but now you're lost."

With such a long detour to examine the importance of patience, you might think that I've run off and left you, that you're lost. Rest assured, I know where you are. You're sitting on a lofty perch atop Mount Compassion, where you've just rescued the value of compassion from adult brats. As you pause to marvel at the stunning view of the territory you've traversed, you also realize you can see the finish line down in the valley below. The trip is almost over. With your backpack loaded with honesty, loyalty, and compassion, you sense that the rest of your journey is downhill, a piece of cake. But after reading this chapter, you know it isn't. It's the part of your journey when the last gasp of the hideous strength tries to stop you from claiming complete victory over its children, if only it can get you to lose your patience.

I believe you won't. You've managed to stay with me on this journey thus far and you will complete it; you're no Jack Butler.

I believe that whatever wisdom is contained in these pages, you're going to use it to fight against the growing personal immaturity that exists in your workplace.

I believe this because, like Art Rollins, you are tired of the foolishness that threatens the institution that provides you the food you eat, the vehicle you drive, and the retirement resources that you depend on. And I believe this because your arsenal of understanding that equips you to fight the good fight against adult brats is much larger than when you began this journey with me.

You now know the depth to which the problems created by adult brats can sink your business or organization. If you don't, then simply turn on the news and witness what's happened to the American economy thanks to a cadre of adult brats who felt they could do what they pleased without accountability.

You now know what the adult brat culprit looks like. It isn't the coworker whose personal habits simply annoy you. It's someone whose life view is much more problematic, someone who's steeped in self-destruction because the emotional bonding that defines healthy relational beings is missing.

You now know what social forces give rise to adult brats and keep them empowered to wreak havoc, stealing from your workplace the values of honesty, loyalty, and compassion. You also now know how to use transparency, accountability, and incorruptibility to wrestle them back from the thieves.

No, you won't lose patience. You'll finish the job. And if I should visit you at your place of work, you will be able to show me your adult brat-free workplace. I'd like that.

I have this faith because you know where you are on the map. You're not lost. You're at the finish line, and it is time for us to each go our own way.

May your journey be bountiful.

Notes

Chapter One: Help! I'm Surrounded by Jerks!

1. David Rattray, ed., *The Reader's Digest Illustrated Encyclopedia Dictionary* (Boston: Houghton Mifflin, 1987), 300.

Chapter Two: Selling Us Out

1. Cheryl Hall, "No Jerks Need Apply at SPM Communications," *Dallas Morning News*, March 12, 2008.
2. Rick Jolly, *Jackspeak: A Guide to British Naval Slang and Usage* (Liskeard, England: Maritime Books, 2000), http://www.torontojobsource.com/witwisdom.htm.
3. Alan Finder, "For Some, Online Persona Undermines a Resume," *New York Times*, June 11, 2006.
4. Jacquielynn Floyd, "If Guilty, Teacher Would Be Latest to Dishonor Classroom," *Dallas Morning News*, June 7, 2006, http://www.dallasnews.com/sharedcontent/dws/dn/local news/columnists/jfloyd/stories/DNfloyd_07met.ART.North. Edition1.18753f25.html.
5. Hudson Employment Index, "One in Three Workers Witness Ethical Misconduct Despite Clearly Communicated Guidelines: Hudson Survey Highlights Gap between Policies and Reality," October 19, 2005, http://www.hudson-index .com/node.asp?SID=5337.
6. US Bureau of Labor Statistics, "Employment Situation Summary," December 2008, http://www.bls.gov/news.release/ empsit.nr0.htm.

7. Hudson Employment Index, "One in Three Workers Witness Ethical Misconduct."

8. Harris Interactive, Harris Poll 38, "Many U.S. Employees Have Negative Attitudes to Their Jobs, Employers and Top Managers," May 6, 2005, http://www.harrisinteractive.com /harris_poll/index.asp?PID=568.

9. US Bureau of Labor Statistics, "Employment Situation Summary."

Chapter Three: A Dark Heart

1. Marc Hansen, "Criminal Past Isn't Deal Killer at I-80 Re-Entry Job Fair," *Des Moines Register*, March 1, 2008, http://cpiboard .wikidot.com/articles.

2. Robert M. Taylor and Lucile P. Morrison. *Taylor-Johnson Temperament Analysis Manual* (Thousand Oaks, CA: Psychological Publications, 1992), 12.

3. "Man Sues IBM for $5 Million after Being Fired for Visiting Adult Chat Room at Work," Associated Press news release, February 17, 2007, http://www.foxnews.com /printer_friendly _story/0,3566,252588,00.html.

4. Ibid.

5. *Taylor-Johnson Temperament Analysis Manual*, 12.

6. Erik Hedegaard, "Matthew Fox Is Not Who You Think He Is," *Men's Journal*, February 2007, 58.

7. Ibid.

8. "Only One in Three Employees Engaged," BlessingWhite press release, April 24, 2008, http://www.blessingwhite.com/doc Description.asp?id=229&pid=6&sid=1.

9. Jean Twenge, *Generation Me* (New York: Free Press, 2006), 6–7.

10. James C. Berbiglia, *The AWOL Syndrome* (Los Angeles: Psychological Publications, 1971), 5.

11. "Only One in Three Employees Engaged."

12. Richard Durrett, "Botts Wants out of Texas Rangers Organization," *Dallas Morning News*, April 30, 2008,

http://www.dallasnews.com/sharedcontent/dws/spt/baseball
/rangers /stories/043008dnsporangbriefs.3c4c656.html.

13. Walter Lippmann, "An Image of Man for Liberal Democracy," *Commonweal*, December 30, 1941, http://www.podmonkeyx .com/Walter_Lippmann/article.asp?articleID=25.

14. Ibid.

15. Richard Siklos, "Conrad Black's Shabby Downfall," CNNMoney.com, December 10, 2007, http://cnnmoney.print this.clickability.com/pt/cpt?action=cpt&title=Co..._black .fortune percent2Findex.htm percent3Fpostversion percent3 D2007121018&partnerID=2200.

16. Richard Siklos, "Conrad Black's Downfall Shaped by Many Battles," *New York Times*, July 14, 2007, http://www.nytimes .com/2007/07/14/business/14react.html?_r=1&hp=&oref =slogin&pagewanted=print.

Chapter Four: Why Jerks Exist

1. "Report to the Nations on Occupational Fraud and Abuse," Association of Certified Fraud Examiners, 2014, http://www .acfe.com/rttn/docs/2014-report-to-nations.pdf.

2. Frank E. Bird Jr. and George L. Germain, *Practical Loss Control Leadership* (Loganville, GA: International Loss Control Institute, 1985), 63.

3. Ibid.

4. Virginia Reza, "After 40 Years, Air Defender Says Goodbye," *Monitor*, February 15, 2007, 39.

5. Ibid.

6. Lolita C. Baldor, "Poorly Behaved Soldiers Promoted," Associated Press, April 29, 2008, http://www.time.com/time /nation/article/0,8599,1736027,00.html.

7. Josh Daniel, in discussion with the author, February 2008.

8. Henry M. Paulson Jr., *The Department of the Treasury Blueprint for a Modernized Financial Regulatory Structure* (Washington, DC: US Department of the Treasury, March 2008), 18.

9. Jennifer S. Lee, "For Insurance: Adult Children Ride Piggyback," *New York Times*, September 17, 2008, http://query.nytimes .com/gst/fullpage.html?res=9F01E4D81331F934A2575AC 0A9609C8B63&scp=1&sq=Jennifer+S.+Lee+Piggyback &st=nyt.

10. David Brooks, "The Great Seduction," *New York Times*, June 10, 2008, http://www.nytimes.com/2008/06/10/opinion /10brooks .html?_r=1&oref=slogin.

11. Jean Twenge, *Generation Me* (New York: Free Press, 2006), 57.

12. Ibid.

13. Ibid.

14. Emily Meehan, "New Grads Are Impatient for Promotion," *Wall Street Journal Online Edition*, June 20, 2007, http:// online. wsj.com/article/SB118229562734041231.html.

15. Michael Alison Chandler, "VA Student's Snow-Day Plea Triggers an Online Storm," *Washington Post*, January 23, 2008, http://www.washingtonpost.com/wp-dyn/content/article /2008/01/22/AR2008012203660_Comments.html.

16. Ibid.

17. Betsy Israel, "The Overconnecteds," *New York Times*, November 5, 2006, http://www.nytimes.com/2006/11/05/education/edlife/ connect.html...5087 percent0A&em=&en =ca1b145d96058b3e &ex=1163048400&pagewanted=print.

18. Ibid.

19. Christopher Maag, "A Hoax Turned Fatal Draws Anger but No Charges," *New York Times*, November 28, 2007, http://www.nytimes.com/2007/11/28/us/28hoax.html?ei =5087&em=&e...l=1&adxnnlx=1196344993-NbqCHS86ASO EtIxDunorlg&pagewanted=print.

20. Michael Bugeja, "Facing the Facebook," *Chronicle Careers*, January 23, 2006, http://chronicle.com/jobs/news/2006/01 /2006012301c.htm.

21. Jim Reeves, "To Contend, Texas Rangers Need Their Ace," *Fort Worth Star-Telegram*, July 2, 2008, http://www.star-telegram .com/sports/story/736472.html.

22. Stephanie Armour, "Business Casual Causes Confusion," *USA Today*, July 9, 2007, http://www.usatoday.com/money/work place/2007-07-09-business-casual-attire_n.htm.

23. Clarence Page, "TV's Bad-Guy Businessmen," *Chicago Tribune Online Edition*, July 19, 2006, http://www.chicagotribune .com/news/columnists/chi-0607190148jul19,1,1234783 .column?coll=chi-newscol.

24. Ibid.

25. Suzanne Miller in discussion with the author, August 2008.

26. Gregory Acs and Sandi Nelson, *The Kids Are Alright? Children's Well-Being and the Rise in Cohabitation*, Urban Institute, series B, no. B-48, July 2002, http://www.urban.org /publications/310544.html.

27. Ibid.

28. April Clark, Cary Funk, and Paul Taylor, *As Marriage and Parenthood Drift Apart, Public Is Concerned about Social Impact*, Pew Research Center, July 1, 2007, http://pewsocial trends.org/pubs/526/marriage-parenthood/.

29. Ibid.

30. Ibid.

31. Stephen E. Ambrose, *Undaunted Courage* (New York: Simon & Schuster, 1996), 226–227.

Chapter Five: Encouraging the Jerk Mentality

1. C. S. Lewis, *That Hideous Strength* (New York: Scribner, 1996).

2. R. Roger, "Is it time to read . . . That Hideous Strength?" The Inklings blog, August 9, 2007, http://oxfordinklings.blogspot .com/2007/08/is-it-time-to-read-that-hideous.html.

3. Maryclaire Dale, "Lawyer: 2 Will Admit Fraud Fueled Luxury Lifestyle," Star-Telegram.com, May 13, 2008, http://www .star-telegram.com/466/story/638380.html.

4. Joseph A. Gambardello, "Poster Child for ID Theft," *Philadelphia Inquirer*, May 13, 2008, http://www.philly.com

/inquirer/home_top_left_story/20080513__Poster_children __for_ID _theft.html.

5. Kay S. Hymowitz, "Child-Man in the Promised Land," *City Journal* 18, no. 1 (winter 2008), http://www.city-journal .org/2008/18_1_single_young_men.html.

6. Emily Meehan, "Taking Time off to Travel," *Wall Street Journal Online Edition*, March 7, 2007, http://online.wsj.com/article _print/SB117320946106328528.html.

7. Trey Garrison, "Death of an SMU Co-Ed," *D Magazine*, April 2008, March 19, 2008, http://www.dmagazine.com/ME2 /Apps/PublishingMultiselect/Print.asp?Module=Publishing Titles&id=0E50A9E7232642E08168B7413A70015F.

8. David Brooks, "The Rank-Link Imbalance," *New York Times*, March 14, 2008, http://www.nytimes.com/2008/03/14/opinion /14brooks.html.

9. Sue Shellenbarger, "When 20-Somethings Move Back Home, It Isn't All Bad," *Wall Street Journal Online Edition*, May 21, 2008, http://online.wsj.com/article/SB121130668211207625.html.

10. Ibid.

11. Kelli Renfrow, "Cutting the Cord Means More than Moving Out," *Dallas Morning News*, September 21, 2006, http:// www.dallasnews.com/sharedcontent/dws/fea/family/stories /DN-NFM_renfrow_0921liv.ART.State.Edition1.3eb0f2e .html, emphasis added.

12. Ian Urbina, "With Parents Absent: Trying to Keep Child Care in the Family," *New York Times*, July 23, 2006, http:// query.nytimes.com/gst/fullpage.html?res=9806E4DC143FF 930A15754C0A9609C8B63.

13. Jason Deparle, "Life after Welfare: The Grandmothers; As Welfare Rolls Shrink, Load on Relatives Grows," February 21, 1999, *New York Times*, http://query.nytimes.com/gst /fullpage .html?res=9C02EEDE123DF932A15751C0A96F9582 60.

14. US Department of Health and Human Services, "Foster Care Statistics 2013," April 2015, https://www.childwelfare.gov /pubs/factsheets/foster/.

15. Gina Kolata, "Study Says Chatty Doctors Forget Patients," *New York Times*, June 26, 2007, http://www.nytimes .com/2007/06/26/health/26doctors.html?_r=1&scp=1&sq =Chatty percent20Doctors&st=cse&oref=slogin.
16. Ibid.
17. Steve Chawkins, "Judge Snubs Victim's Kin's Plea for Mercy," *Los Angeles Times Online Edition*, January 27, 2007, http:// articles.latimes.com/2007/jan/27/local/me-mercy27.
18. Sue Shellenbarger, "Read This and Weep: Crying at Work Gains Acceptance," *Wall Street Journal Online Edition*, April 26, 2007, http://online.wsj.com/article/SB1177540506357826 43.html.
19. Ibid.
20. Ibid.
21. Cleve Wiese, "Friends Came to Know Two Sides of Woodson," *Richmond Times-Dispatch*, March 29, 2008, http://www. richmond.com/news/article_eda475de-b2cc-5863-988b-34dda25fab9f.html.
22. "Japanese Firm Creates Robot Girlfriend for Lonely Men," Fox News.com, June 18, 2008, http://www.foxnews.com /story/0,2933,368282,00.html.

Chapter Six: Using Guile and Guts

1. Wade Goodwyn, "The Perilous Path of FAA Whistle-Blowers," National Public Radio, September 10, 2008, http://www.npr .org/templates/story/story.php?storyid =91428378.
2. Ibid.
3. S. Truett Cathy, Speech to The Leader Board, Dallas Theological Seminary, September 9, 2008. My notes are from my audio recording of the speech. The Leader Board is an educational function of the Howard G. Hendricks Center for Christian Leadership at Dallas Theological Seminary.
4. Debbie Sardone, in discussion with the author, September 16, 2008.

5. Francis Brown, S. R. Driver, Charles A. Briggs, and William Gesenius, "Hebrew Lexicon entry for Nokach," *NAS Old Testament Lexicon*, http://www.biblestudytools.net/Lexicons /Hebrew/heb.cgi?number=5227&version=kjv.

Chapter Seven: Restoring Workplace Accountability

1. Benedict Carey, "Citizen Enforcers Take Aim," *New York Times*, October 7, 2008.
2. Walter Lippmann, "An Image of Man for Liberal Democracy," *Commonweal*, December 30, 1941, http://www.podmonkeyx .com/Walter_Lippmann/article.asp?articleID=25.
3. Carey, "Citizen Enforcers Take Aim."
4. Jim Collins, *Good to Great* (New York: HarperCollins Publishers, 2001).
5. David Brooks, "The Testing Time," *New York Times*, October 7, 2008.

Chapter Eight: Teaching Corruption-Busting Compassion

1. Carl Schurz, "Abraham Lincoln: An Essay by Carl Schurz" (1899), in *The Writings of Abraham Lincoln*, vol. 1, ed. Arthur Brooks Lapsley, http://www.gutenberg.org/etext/3253.
2. Jason M. Kanov et al., "Compassion in Organizational Life," *American Behavioral Scientist* 47 (2004): 808–827.
3. George Will, "Getting Sensitive to the Therapeutic Ethos of Politics," *Dallas Morning News*, February 8, 1999.
4. Kanov et al., "Compassion in Organizational Life," 808–827.
5. Quoted in Kevin Sherrington, "Coaches Provide Healing Touch," *Dallas Morning News*, August 8, 2004.
6. Erin McKean, ed., *Oxford American Dictionary* (New York: Oxford University Press, 2006), 183.

7. Jack Deere, *Surprised by the Power of the Spirit* (Grand Rapids, MI: Zondervan, 1993), 279–280.

8. Hampton Keathley IV, "The Miracles of Jesus," Biblical Studies Foundation, 1996, 18, http://www.bible.org/page.asp·age_id =2218.

Acknowledgments

For the pleasure of writing about the wilderness journeys that teach us about human nature at work, I am thankful to many. First, my thanks goes belatedly to my mentors, the late James M. "Mike" Reese, who first saw in me the potential to help troubled kids, and to Howard G. Hendricks, for pointing the way to wilderness camping as a vehicle to help them.

I am deeply indebted to my early comrades and covisionaries in Wilderness Encounter Programs—Glen Riddle, Dave George, Wayne Hower, and Tom Williams—who deserve equal credit for both birthing a difficult (at best) camp program and keeping it operating during lean financial times. The tough, often cold and fitful nights on the trail I shared with you are among the highlights of my life. Along with us were the many trip counselors who sacrificed body, soul, and (sometimes) paycheck to help troubled kids and their families. You have my undying admiration and thanks.

To Tom Haralson, my former business partner, I owe a debt of gratitude for helping open the doors of business to the application of the principles in this book. Arnie Rothstein, Larry Rigdon, and Doug Taylor are businessmen who first allowed Tom and me to challenge their employees to reject adult brathood; to them and to the late Bob Millard I am grateful.

I'm also thankful that Leslie Nunn Reed, literary agent, and Eric Stanford, editor, lent their support and expertise to the crafting of this book. Without Leslie's encouragement to proactively approach publishers with the concept of *No Jerks on the Job*, I'd still be floundering in thoughts without words. And without Eric's skillful editing of my initial manuscript, I'd sound like the dumb "wilderness jock" who lurks close beneath my pseudointellectual soul.

Finally, to Melanie, my wife, I express my deepest love and thanks. Your unquestioned support of a crazy camp ministry that took me away from home and out of communication range while you reared our children is a loving sacrifice that I will never forget. When it came time to write about the fruits of that sacrifice, you not only encouraged me, you served as my capable frontline editor. I'm amazed at your plethora of skills. I pray that the benefit the readers receive from this, our book, will sustain us for years to come.

Index

A

Absent without leave (AWOL), 36–38, 65

Accountability, 124–128, 138–139
  external, 124, 126–128, 135, 138
  formula for, 138
  hupodikos, 125
  and loyalty, 131, 137
  personal, 125–126, 128, 138
  purpose of, 139
  versus revenge, 124, 126

Adams, George, 20

Adolescence:
  adulthood, battle between, 75–76
  definition of, 75
  media portrayal of, 77–80
  normal, 77–80
  prolonged, 75–77

Adolescents-at-work syndrome, 20–22, 55–56

Adult brats at work, x–xi, 5–6. *See also* Jerks on the job
  causes of, social, 47–69
  characteristics, 47–49

compared to juvenile delinquents, 25–26, 31–38
  absent without leave (AWOL), 36–38, 65
  emotional detachment, 33–36, 65
  self-destructiveness, 31–33, 65
confrontation of, 138–139
contributing factors:
  personal, 50, 71, 74
  system, 50
description of, 29
and deviance, 11, 19, 25–26, 38, 59
identifying, 43–45
loyalty, misplaced, 113–114
model, causation, 49–50
preconceptions of, avoiding, 175–176
the problem:
  denying, 25
  recognizing, 25–26